Classroom Instruction
that works
with English Language Learners

Jane D. Hill • Kathleen M. Flynn

Association for Supervision and Curriculum Development
Alexandria, Virginia USA

Association for Supervision and Curriculum Development
1703 N. Beauregard St. Alexandria, VA 22311-1714 USA
Phone: 800-933-2723 or 703-578-9600 Fax: 703-575-5400
Web site: www.ascd.org E-mail: member@ascd.org
Author guidelines: www.ascd.org/write

Gene R. Carter, *Executive Director*; Nancy Modrak, *Director of Publishing*; Julie Houtz, *Director of Book Editing & Production*; Ernesto Yermoli, *Project Manager*; Cathy Guyer, *Senior Graphic Designer*; Valerie Younkin, *Desktop Publishing Specialist*; Vivian Coss, *Production Specialist*

ASCD Member Book, No. FY07-01 (September 2006, PCR). ASCD Member Books mail to Premium (P), Comprehensive (C), and Regular (R) members on this schedule: Jan., PC; Feb., P; Apr., PCR; May, P; July, PC; Aug., P; Sept., PCR; Nov., PC; Dec., P.

PAPERBACK ISBN-13: 978-1-4166-0390-0 ASCD product #106009

PAPERBACK ISBN-10: 1-4166-0390-5

Also available as an e-book through ebrary, netLibrary, and many online booksellers (see Books in Print for the ISBNs).

Quantity discounts for the paperback edition only: 10–49 copies, 10%; 50+ copies, 15%; for 1,000 or more copies, call 800-933-2723, ext. 5634, or 703-575-5634. For desk copies: member@ascd.org.

Library of Congress Cataloging-in-Publication Data

Hill, Jane, 1953–
    Classroom instruction that works with English language learners / Jane Hill and Kathleen Flynn.
        p. cm.
    Includes bibliographical references and index.
    ISBN-13: 978-1-4166-0390-0 (pbk. alk. paper)
    ISBN-10: 1-4166-0390-5 (pbk. alk. paper) 1. Linguistic minorities—Education—United States. 2. English language—Study and teaching—Foreign speakers. 3. Language and education—United States. 4. Communication in education—United States. 5. Mainstreaming in education—United States. I. Flynn, Kathleen, 1963– II. Title.
    LC3731.H554 2006
    428.2'4—dc22
                                                                    2006014599

15 14 13 12 11 10 09 08 07 06   1 2 3 4 5 6 7 8 9 10 11 12

To my husband, Rocky Hill.
—Jane

To Kiley and Caitlin, who bring light into my life,
and to Hailey, the newest star in the constellation.
—Kathleen

Classroom Instruction *that works* *with* English Language Learners

Foreword vii

Acknowledgments x

Preface xii

Introduction 1

Chapter 1: What Is *Classroom Instruction That Works?*. 5

Chapter 2: The Stages of Second Language Acquisition 14

Chapter 3: Setting Objectives and Providing Feedback 22

Chapter 4: Nonlinguistic Representations 36

Chapter 5: Cues, Questions, and Advance Organizers 44

Chapter 6: Cooperative Learning 55

Chapter 7: Summarizing and Note Taking 62

Chapter 8: Homework and Practice 77

Chapter 9: Reinforcing Effort and Providing Recognition 87

Chapter 10: Generating and Testing Hypotheses 95

Chapter 11: Identifying Similarities and Differences 101

Chapter 12: Involving Parents and the Community 111

Conclusion 118

Appendix A: Types of Graphic Organizers 121

Appendix B: Types of Summary Frames 123

Appendix C: Example of a Three-Year
Parent and Community Involvement Plan 127

References 132

Index 137

About the Authors 143

FOREWORD

It should come as no surprise to readers of this book that many English language learners (ELLs) are enrolled in U.S. public schools today. Moreover, it should be no shock to learn that this population is continually expanding. There are ELLs in all 50 states—from Alaska to Arizona, from Connecticut to California—as well as in Puerto Rico, the Virgin Islands, and Guam. These students speak a variety of languages and come from diverse social, cultural, and economic backgrounds. There are greater numbers of ELLs in the states that have historically been affected by them, but there are also many in states that until very recently had none.

The No Child Left Behind Act (NCLB) calls for quality education and accountability for all children in U.S. schools. If the rhetoric of NCLB is to become a reality, the phrase "all means all" must be applied to include ELLs as well as other populations of U.S. students.

Ironically, it seems that the more diverse our schools become, the greater the pressure to homogenize the curriculum and instruction. For ELLs, this pressure has meant fewer opportunities to learn in bilingual and English as a second language (ESL) classrooms. For teachers, increased diversity has meant a stronger push to teach English quickly and place ELLs in mainstream classrooms.

There is an urgent need to improve the quantity and quality of instruction for ELLs, both in special programs and in basic classrooms. All teachers of ELLs, and those in mainstream classrooms in particular, are searching for effective teaching strategies for these students. This book makes a crucial contribution to the field by providing solid information and ideas for teaching ELLs. These ideas can be implemented in mainstream classes that are heterogeneous with regard to language, ethnicity, social class, and academic achievement. This book also proposes that second language learning is a long-term process that must be considered in instructional planning over the span of many school years and in multiple curricular contexts.

Among the many strengths of this book is its acknowledgment of the diversity of the ELL population without presenting it as a problem to be solved. The authors do not homogenize ELLs by lumping them into one generic group, but instead exhort teachers to learn about these students, their languages, their heritages, and their interests. This book also honors parents, and places the responsibility for parent involvement in the hands of school districts and school leaders as well as individual teachers.

The tone of this book reflects a respect for classroom teachers and their expertise, and engages them in the quest to develop and implement innovative instructional programs for ELLs. This book also makes a very strong case that caring and compassionate mainstream teachers can and should be part of the team working to ensure equitable and effective learning opportunities for the nation's ELLs.

The structure of this book and the strategies it presents demonstrate that rigor in the education of these students is important, but so, too, is realism. This book strikes a nice balance between the condescending *pobrecitos* syndrome so often heard in schools, which implies that ELLs can't learn much in regular classrooms, and the viewpoint at the opposite extreme, which holds that good teachers can accelerate the language development of ELLs significantly in a single school year. Both of these perspectives cause teachers to throw up their hands in frustration.

The tone of this book is compassionate and empathetic toward the students and their families who, for many reasons, have found themselves in strange new communities and classrooms. The authors innately understand that ELLs must overcome many difficult challenges in the classroom, and they acknowledge the fact that these students deserve to be taught by teachers who are skillful and caring.

Fortunately, this book succeeds in providing balance, solid advice, information, and guidance that will help both ELLs and their teachers feel competent and confident in the classroom. Kudos to the authors for their commonsense approach, and for their respectful treatment of ELLs as emerging bilinguals who have linguistic and cultural strengths that should be used and appreciated in schools.

This book offers concrete suggestions for teachers without reducing the teaching of ELLs to trite and overused rhetoric that suggests that "good teaching is simply good teaching." The integrity of demonstrating the complexities of second language learning while at the same time reassuring teachers that they can be effective with ELLs is useful and provides encouragement to teachers who find themselves teaching children they were not formally prepared to teach.

—Kathy Escamilla, PhD
University of Colorado at Boulder

ACKNOWLEDGMENTS

We acknowledge the following K–6 content area teachers, who contributed to this book by sharing how the *Classroom Instruction That Works* strategies worked with English language learners in their classrooms:

- Elisabeth Berry, Denise Hitchcock, and Lindsey Moses of North Elementary School, Brighton, Colorado;
- Cecilia Bailey, William Gibson, and Jolene Smith of Kayenta Intermediate School, Kayenta, Arizona; and
- Sheri Daigler, Sandra Drechsler, Kelly Gardner, Amy Libertini, Adam Schmucker, and Eliza Sorte of Berry Creek Middle School, Edwards, Colorado.

We also thank Sylvia Torrez, senior consultant at Mid-continent Research for Education and Learning (McREL), who contributed classroom examples to illustrate how to ask tiered questions and stimulate language in various content areas.

We extend our deep gratitude to McREL's senior director of product development, Adrienne Schure, who guided the development process and was our cheerleader. Other McREL staff to whom we are grateful include Brian Lancaster, Doug Lockwood, Sally Grubb, and Susan Adams.

We especially thank Barbara Barr and Liz Grassi for their valuable feedback on this book.

*   *   *

This book has been funded in part with federal funds from the Southwest Comprehensive Center, which is part of the national network of 15 centers funded by Title XIII of the Elementary and Secondary Education Act of 1965, as amended by continuing legislation.

PREFACE

After analyzing demographic data from the 2000 census, demographer Harold Hodgkinson (2003) found that almost 9 million U.S. children between the ages of 5 and 17 speak a language other than English at home, and a full 2.6 million of them do not speak English well. Hodgkinson estimated that in 2000, almost half a million children under the age of 5 were being raised in homes where no English was spoken at all. At least 125,000 of these children were likely to need special help in preschool and kindergarten in order to learn to speak and read English. If they do not get that help in their early years (and often they do not), it will be up to our elementary school teachers to teach academic content as well as proficiency in English. As many of you already know, this is not an easy task.

English language learners (ELLs) may once have been viewed as "belonging" to English as a second language (ESL) staff, but now, due to changing laws and policies, they are in every classroom in the school, making the job of teaching that much more challenging. Most elementary classroom teachers have not been trained to help students master content standards *and* language standards, as ELLs must do. Although many of you have probably already turned to colleagues, books, the Internet, and other resources for help, you are still essentially on your own in learning how to help your ELLs succeed.

We have written this book to specifically provide you with strategies and tactics designed to address the needs of ELLs. Using the research from *Classroom Instruction That Works* (Marzano, Pickering, & Pollock, 2001)—itself a summary of findings from over 100 studies—we review nine categories of research-based instructional strategies that strongly affect student achievement. We examine these strategies in depth, and also look at the existing research on modifying these strategies for use with ELLs. When no relevant research exists on a given strategy, we rely on the generalizations from the research and the classroom recommendations from *Classroom Instruction That Works*. To that we add professional wisdom that comes from our experiences as ESL teachers and trainers.

This book has two goals. The first is to provide you, the mainstream classroom teacher, with background knowledge on instructional strategies and practices that have been positively linked to student achievement. The second is to show you how these strategies can be modified to help ELLs acquire content and language skills. We sincerely hope this book will help make the job of reaching and teaching your steadily increasing population of ELLs less difficult and more rewarding.

INTRODUCTION

Language is the air that we breathe and the water in which we swim. It comes as naturally to us as seeing the sky or digesting our food. It is as vital a part of us as our name and personality. But what if we suddenly had to breathe different air or swim in different waters? What if we consciously had to think about selecting the words we were going to say, getting them in the right order, applying the correct grammatical rules, and using the correct pronunciation? If we had to think about not only what we say but also how to say it, the language overload would be exhausting.

Think about a time when you traveled to a place where English was not the dominant language. Remember how you felt when you returned home and heard English for the first time since you had left? What did you feel? Relief? Safety? Comfort? Friendship? We *are* our language.

In addition, language has always been the medium of instruction: As teachers, our automatic use of English helps us to create or produce something new for students. We can create stories, produce explanations, construct meaning when we read, and help students make meaningful connections—all by just opening our mouths. Although we may have to deliberately concentrate on classroom management or what activity we will do next, we are not thinking about the order of words in our next sentence.

With the influx of English language learners (ELLs) in mainstream classrooms today, however, the comfortable, automatic sense of "just talking" is being shaken up. What we previously did not have to think about, we now have to think about very carefully. We suddenly find ourselves having to accommodate the one thing we take for granted: language. We are experienced accommodators when it comes to rates of learning, behaviors, and modes of response. We can accommodate anything, from students with special education needs to those with hygienic needs, but up until recently we have not had to make accommodations for language.

Aside from accommodating for students with violent tendencies, accommodating for language is one of the most difficult tasks we face as mainstream teachers. To teach students a new language is to help them know its sounds (phonology), its words (lexicon), and its sentence formation (syntax and semantics). To help students learn content in a new language, we must use clear and concise articulation, make eye contact, use visuals, employ gestures/body movement/pantomime, use shorter and simpler sentences at a slower rate, use high-frequency vocabulary, and eliminate idiomatic expressions. We also have to model, scaffold, access, and activate students' prior knowledge; provide cooperative learning activities; and differentiate instruction. Making such accommodations helps provide better instruction for all of your students.

A Growing Challenge for Mainstream Teachers

The number of ELLs attending U.S. schools has grown dramatically over the past 25 years, and it appears that this number will continue to increase. Between 1979 and 2003, the overall number of school-age children (ages 5–17) increased by 19 percent. However, during this same time period, the number of children who spoke a language other than English at home increased by 161 percent; of those, the number who spoke English with difficulty (i.e., less than "very well") grew by 124 percent. Overall, 5.5 percent of the school-age population in the United States speaks a language other than English at home and speaks English with difficulty, but this number varies when the nation is broken down by region. Regional percentages range from 8.7 percent in the West to 3.2 percent in the South (U.S. Department of Education, National Center for Education Statistics, 2005).

Teaching English language skills to ELLs is now the responsibility of all school staff. We used to think that the English as a second language (ESL) teacher would take care of everything. Perhaps we even encouraged classroom teachers to leave this kind of teaching to the specialists, much as we did with students in pullout special education programs. After all, the reasoning went, there are federally funded programs for this special segment of the population. Along with the federal dollars come separate services with special materials, classrooms, teachers, and program directors.

But now, just as we have been told we need to include special education students in our mainstream classrooms (without being told how to accomplish this feat), we are also facing the integration of growing numbers of ELLs. According to the National Clearinghouse for English Language Acquisition (n.d.a), English language learners represent the fastest growing segment of the school-age population. At this moment, the greatest effect is being felt in elementary schools.

This book is intended to offer help for elementary school mainstream teachers who have ELLs in their classrooms for all or part of the instructional day. Forty-four percent of all ELLs in U.S. public schools are currently in grades preK–3 (Education Market Research Corner Archives, 2004). However, schools and teachers will need to be prepared to teach these students as they get older.

English language learners present many challenges for mainstream teachers. No two ELLs have the same amount of grounding in their native language, or are at the same stage of English language acquisition. The language skills of these students vary, making for even greater complexity. Some students are born in the United States but grow up in non-English-speaking households; others arrive in the classroom having received varying amounts of formal education in their country of birth. Still others may have been in U.S. schools for a number of years, but may still be in the early stages of English language acquisition. The students' levels of exposure to English, their educational histories, the socioeconomic levels of their families, and the number of books in their homes all play a role in their readiness to learn—and learn *in*—a new language.

Over the past few years, staff members at Mid-continent Research for Education and Learning have worked with mainstream teachers in a small rural district in Wyoming, training them in instructional strategies for ELLs. In the course of this training, author Jane Hill turned to *Classroom Instruction That Works* (Marzano, Pickering, & Pollock, 2001) and found that she instinctively recognized some of the strategies presented in this book. As an ESL specialist, she had been recommending some of the strategies to teachers for years. She began to wonder whether some of the strategies had been drawn from the literature on ESL instruction or whether it was the other way around. Had experts in second-language learning taken strategies that had proven effective with English- dominant students and adapted them to meet the needs of second language learners based on their level of English proficiency and background knowledge?

Jane's curiosity was piqued. How many of the research-based strategies for increasing student achievement in *Classroom Instruction That Works* had been tried with ELLs? How did the strategies need to be modified for the unique instructional needs of these students?

In searching for answers to these questions, we wrote this book, which offers instructional strategies based on research and practical experience that will help you, as a mainstream teacher, include your ELLs in activities with English-dominant students. We examine the strategies from *Classroom Instruction That Works*, discuss any relevant studies, and provide examples of how to adapt the strategies for ELLs based on their level of English language acquisition. We also provide comments from K–6 mainstream teachers who are currently using these strategies in classrooms that contain both ELLs and English-dominant students.

After learning that *Classroom Instruction That Works* was written for all students at all grade levels, you might question how the strategies can be implemented; you may know you have to differentiate for ELLs, but maybe you're unsure about how to make it happen. This book serves as a supplement to *Classroom Instruction That Works*. With it, we examine each category and, whenever possible, suggest differentiation using two formulas: tiered questions and a strategy known as Word-MES (language stimulation through word selection, modeling English, expanding knowledge of English, and developing academic English so that students begin to "sound like a book"). These two formulas present content to ELLs while concurrently fostering their language development. (They can even be used with English-dominant students who come to the classroom with limited vocabulary and grammatical skills.)

Further explanations of tiered questions and Word-MES are presented throughout this book, especially in Chapter 2. As you read, you may nod your head as you come across strategies and modifications you are already employing. Confirmation for what you are currently doing is a good thing. We hope you also learn new strategies to implement, and that you come to view your ELLs as students on a journey to discover new knowledge in a new language.

1

WHAT IS *CLASSROOM INSTRUCTION THAT WORKS?*

"Research-based" is today's buzzword for teachers when it comes to choosing modes of instruction, curricula, and forms of assessment. Particularly since the advent of the No Child Left Behind Act (NCLB), teachers can no longer rely solely on their knowledge of best practices or their years of experience.

In the late 1990s, researchers at Mid-continent Research for Education and Learning (McREL) were at the forefront of this paradigm shift—a shift, essentially, from viewing teaching as an art toward viewing it as a science. Another shift in educational thinking was under way at the same time: Researchers were realizing that studies from the 1960s and 1970s indicating that school quality accounted for only 10 percent of differences in students' academic performance (Coleman et al., 1966; Jencks et al., 1972) were not entirely accurate. In particular, researchers found that even if a school was not highly effective in raising student performance, individual teachers could still have a powerful effect on students' academic achievement (Brophe & Good, 1986; Sanders & Horn, 1994; Wright, Horn, & Sanders, 1997).

Buoyed by this new line of research, McREL researchers began looking at studies of various instructional strategies that could be used by individual teachers. An instructional strategy was defined as an alterable behavior on the part of teachers or students. Using meta-analysis, these researchers analyzed over 100 studies of instructional strategies, spanning 30 years. (A meta-analysis combines the results of many studies to determine the average effect of a technique or strategy. Because of the large sample size, this is considered an especially strong method of identifying what works in educational practice.) Through its meta-analysis, McREL researchers identified nine categories of instructional strategies that proved to be exceptionally effective in increasing student performance:

- Setting objectives and providing feedback
- Nonlinguistic representations
- Cues, questions, and advance organizers
- Cooperative learning
- Summarizing and note taking
- Homework and practice
- Reinforcing effort and providing recognition
- Generating and testing hypotheses
- Identifying similarities and differences

The results of this research are presented in a practitioner-friendly format in *Classroom Instruction That Works* (Marzano, Pickering, & Pollock, 2001) and the accompanying resource manual, *A Handbook for Classroom Instruction That Works* (Marzano, Norford, Paynter, Pickering, & Gaddy, 2001). *Classroom Instruction That Works* provides an overview of the research on each category, offers generalizations regarding the use of each category, and presents examples of actual classroom implementation of relevant instructional strategies. Before differentiating these strategies for ELLs in detail, we present here a quick overview of each category, including definitions and some generalizations drawn from the research. Discussion of actual instructional practices can be found in subsequent chapters.

If you have already read *Classroom Instruction That Works* and are familiar with the nine categories of instructional strategies, feel free to move right ahead to Chapter 2, where we discuss the process of second language acquisition.

Setting Objectives and Providing Feedback

By setting objectives and providing feedback, teachers give students a direction for learning and offer information on how well they are performing relative to a particular learning goal.

Two main generalizations can be drawn from the research on setting objectives. First, by setting instructional goals, teachers can narrow the focus for students. (Instructional goals should not be too specific, however, or learning will be limited.) Second, students should be encouraged to adapt the teacher's goals to their own personal needs and desires.

The research suggests four generalizations on providing feedback to students:

1. Feedback should be corrective in nature; that is, it should provide students with information on what they are doing correctly and incorrectly.
2. The timeliness of feedback is essential to its effectiveness. Generally, the later feedback is given—after an exam, for example—the lower the improvement in academic achievement.
3. Feedback should be specific to a criterion, meaning it should tell students where they stand relative to a specific academic goal (criterion-referenced feedback) rather than relative to their peers (norm-referenced feedback).
4. Students can effectively provide their own feedback through ongoing self-evaluation of their learning and performance.

Nonlinguistic Representations

The use of nonlinguistic representations enhances students' ability to represent and elaborate on knowledge using mental images. *Classroom Instruction That Works* provides two general statements regarding nonlinguistic representations. First, a variety of activities—including creating graphic representations, making physical models, generating mental pictures, drawing pictures and pictographs, and engaging in kinesthetic activity—produce nonlinguistic representations. Second, when generating nonlinguistic representations, students elaborate on (or add to) their knowledge. This means that students not only understand material better but also recall the knowledge more readily. A teacher can further this process by asking students to explain and justify their nonlinguistic representations.

Cues, Questions, and Advance Organizers

By using cues, questions, and advance organizers, teachers enhance students' ability to retrieve, use, and organize what they already know about a topic. In other words, these techniques help activate prior knowledge.

The research offers four generalizations about cues and questions:

1. Cues and questions should focus on the information that is critical to students' understanding of the topic at hand, rather than on what is unusual or interesting about the topic. Focusing on the unusual may heighten student interest for the moment, but it will also distract from the important information that needs to be grasped.
2. Higher-level questions (i.e., those that require analytic thinking) produce deeper learning than lower-level questions (i.e., those that simply require students to recall or recognize information).
3. Waiting briefly before accepting responses from students increases the depth of the answers, leads to more classroom discussion, and facilitates student-to-student interaction.
4. Teachers can use questions effectively both before and after a learning experience. Using questions before a learning experience helps students develop a framework for processing the information.

A somewhat similar set of generalizations applies to the use of advance organizers:

1. Advance organizers should focus on what is important as opposed to what is unusual.
2. Higher-level advance organizers produce deeper learning than lower-level advance organizers.
3. Advance organizers are most useful to students when the information presented is not well organized.
4. Different types of advance organizers produce different results. There are four types of advance organizers:
   a. *Expository* advance organizers are straightforward descriptions of the new content students will be learning. (The research shows that expository organizers are the most effective of the four types.)
   b. *Narrative* advance organizers are stories.
   c. *Skimming* advance organizers involve focusing on and noting what stands out in headings, subheadings, and highlighted information.
   d. *Graphic* advance organizers visually represent information.

Cooperative Learning

Cooperative learning techniques allow students to interact with each other in groups in ways that enhance their learning. When students work in cooperative groups, they make sense of new knowledge by interacting with others.

Three generalizations can be drawn from the research on cooperative learning:

1. Organizing groups by ability level should be done sparingly. Although homogeneous grouping in general is more effective than no grouping, research has shown that students of lower ability perform worse in homogeneous groups, while students of high ability perform only slightly better. Only students of medium ability show a significant increase in achievement when placed in groups with students of similar ability (Lou et al., 1996).
2. Cooperative groups should be small—three to four members per group is ideal.
3. Cooperative learning techniques are most effective when used consistently and systematically; they work best when used at least once a week. Teachers should ensure, however, that students still have time to practice skills independently.

Summarizing and Note Taking

By teaching summarizing and note-taking techniques, teachers can enhance students' ability to synthesize and organize information in a way that captures the main ideas and supporting details. Both summarizing and note taking help students process information.

Summarizing is primarily about distilling information, finding patterns, filling in the missing parts, and synthesizing the information into a condensed form. There are several generalizations from the research on developing summarizing skills. The research makes clear that students must engage in three activities when effectively summarizing: deleting information, substituting information, and keeping information. Moreover, to successfully engage in these three activities, students must analyze the information at a fairly deep level. Research also indicates that familiarity with the structure of the information being summarized makes the process easier.

Like summarizing, note taking asks students to identify key information and restate that information in their own words. There are three main generalizations we can draw from the research on note taking:

1. The least effective way to take notes is verbatim. Trying to record everything that is heard or read does not give students a chance to synthesize the information presented. This does not mean that students should take limited notes; in fact, the more notes they take, the better. It is important, however, that notes be specific to the learning goals outlined by the teacher.
2. Students should consider notes to be works in progress; they should be regularly reviewed, revised, and added to as a student's grasp of the content grows.
3. Students should use their notes as study guides. A set of clear, well-organized notes can be a powerful tool for test preparation.

Homework and Practice

Assigning students homework and practice extends the learning opportunities for reviewing and applying knowledge and enhances the ability to reach the expected level of proficiency for a skill or process.

Classroom Instruction That Works describes four generalizations on assigning homework:

1. Students in lower grades should be assigned less homework than those at higher grade levels.
2. Parent involvement in homework should be kept to a minimum. Although parents can facilitate homework (by providing a good study space for their child, for example), they should not solve homework problems for the student.
3. Teachers should be clear about the purpose of homework. Is the assignment designed for practice of a new skill, to prepare students for the introduction of new content, or to help students elaborate on already introduced content?
4. Homework is more effective when feedback—be it a grade or written comment—is provided.

There are two generalizations from the research regarding practice. First, a student will not master a skill without a significant amount of practice. In fact, students generally do not reach 80 percent competency until they have practiced a skill at least 24 times (Anderson, 1995; Newell & Rosenbloom, 1981). This is important to remember because the goal of practice is to develop a skill or process so that it can be applied fluently with minimal conscious thought. Second, when practicing, students should adapt and shape what they have learned. The conceptual understanding of a skill should develop during practice. Again, students need multiple opportunities to make continued adaptations as they develop their understanding of the skill they are learning.

Reinforcing Effort and Providing Recognition

By reinforcing effort, teachers enhance students' understanding of the relationship between effort and achievement by addressing attitudes and beliefs about learning. People generally attribute success to one or more of these four factors: ability, effort, other people, and luck. Of these four factors, only effort actually contributes to achievement. Although a belief in ability may appear helpful at first, a task will eventually come along for which you do not believe you have the requisite ability. Sometimes you must accomplish a task alone, in which case belief in other people as a source of success can be limiting. As for belief in luck, what if your luck runs out?

There are two related generalizations from the research on reinforcing effort. First, not all students realize the importance of believing in effort as a means for academic success. Second, students can learn to believe that effort pays off, even if they do not initially hold this belief.

"Providing recognition" refers to providing students with rewards or praise for their accomplishments related to the attainment of a goal. The research offers three generalizations in this category:

1. Rewards do not necessarily have a negative effect on intrinsic motivation.
2. Rewards are most effective when students must reach some standard of performance in order to receive them. For example, offering a reward for merely participating in an activity can diminish intrinsic motivation, whereas a reward that is contingent on successful completion of a task increases intrinsic motivation.
3. Abstract symbolic recognition, such as verbal praise, is more effective than tangible rewards, such as candy or money.

Generating and Testing Hypotheses

There are two generalizations from the research in this category. First, hypothesis generation and testing can be approached in an inductive (specific to general) or deductive (general to specific) manner. The research shows that deductive techniques are generally more effective than inductive techniques. Second, teachers should ask students to clearly explain their hypotheses and conclusions. By explaining their thinking, students deepen their understanding of the principle they are applying. This process can also help clear up misconceptions.

Identifying Similarities and Differences

When students identify similarities and differences in the content they are learning, they make new connections, experience new insights, and correct misconceptions. Engaging in these complex reasoning processes helps students understand content at a deeper level.

Two main generalizations can be drawn from the research on identifying similarities and differences. First, both teacher-directed and student-directed comparison tasks enhance student knowledge. However, if a teacher wants students to focus on specific similarities and differences, direct instruction is best. Second, using graphic or symbolic models (such as Venn diagrams or matrices) to represent similarities and differences enhances students' ability to generate similarities and differences, thus enhancing their understanding of, and ability to use, knowledge.

There are a variety of ways to identify similarities and differences. Four highly effective forms of doing so are comparing, classifying, creating metaphors, and creating analogies. Identifying similarities and differences is implicit in the process of comparing, and it is also critical to classifying. To create a metaphor, a student must make the abstract similarities and differences between two elements concrete. In creating analogies, students identify how two pairs of elements are similar.

Summary

The authors of *Classroom Instruction That Works* acknowledge that many questions remain about the categories discussed in this chapter, despite all the research to date. For the purposes of this book, the key unanswered question is whether the categories of strategies set forth in *Classroom Instruction That Works* are effective with diverse student populations, and with English language learners in particular. Are there ways in which a mainstream teacher with ELL students in her classroom can use these categories to help students acquire English and learn content knowledge? When and how would a mainstream teacher use these strategies? Do the strategies need to be adapted for use with ELLs, and if so, why and how? The following chapters help answer these questions.

2

THE STAGES OF SECOND LANGUAGE ACQUISITION

We have all seen children move through the stages of acquiring their first language—from babbling to one-word utterances, two-word phrases, full sentences, and eventually, complex grammar. Students learning a second language also move through stages. One of the most important things you should know about each of your English language learners (ELLs) is which stage of acquisition they are in. Knowing and understanding the stage and its characteristics are critical for effectively differentiating instruction for these students.

Stephen Krashen and Tracy Terrell first explored stages of second language acquisition in their 1983 book, *The Natural Approach*. Figure 2.1 lists the five stages of language acquisition, along with the characteristics, approximate time frames, and appropriate teacher prompts for each stage.

The Preproduction stage lasts from zero to six months and is also known as "the silent period," because it's likely you won't hear students speak any English at all during this stage. At the next level, Early Production, students begin using single words or two-word phrases, yes/no responses, names, and repetitive language patterns (e.g., "How are you?"). At the Speech Emergence stage, students are able to say simple sentences (e.g., "I walked home"). Eventually, at the Intermediate Fluency stage, students can use sentences of

Figure 2.1
Stages of Second Language Acquisition

Stage	Characteristics	Approximate Time Frame	Teacher Prompts
Preproduction	The student • Has minimal comprehension • Does not verbalize • Nods "Yes" and "No" • Draws and points	0–6 months	• Show me. . . • Circle the. . . • Where is. . . ? • Who has. . . ?
Early Production	The student • Has limited comprehension • Produces one- or two-word responses • Participates using key words and familiar phrases • Uses present-tense verbs	6 months–1 year	• Yes/no questions • Either/or questions • One- or two-word answers • Lists • Labels
Speech Emergence	The student • Has good comprehension • Can produce simple sentences • Makes grammar and pronunciation errors • Frequently misunderstands jokes	1–3 years	• Why. . . ? • How. . . ? • Explain. . . • Phrase or short-sentence answers
Intermediate Fluency	The student • Has excellent comprehension • Makes few grammatical errors	3–5 years	• What would happen if. . . ? • Why do you think. . . ?
Advanced Fluency	The student has a near-native level of speech.	5–7 years	• Decide if. . . • Retell. . .

Source: Adapted from Krashen and Terrell (1983).

increasing length and complexity, until finally, at the Advanced Fluency stage, they demonstrate a near-native level of fluency.

All students acquiring English will pass through these stages. Although Figure 2.1 provides an approximate time frame for each stage, the length of time students spend at each level will be as varied as the students themselves. Krashen and Terrell's early work linked classroom activities with the stages to ensure that teachers did not expect utterances from ELLs that were beyond or beneath their stages of acquisition. Imagine, for example, a student in the Preproduction stage being asked "how" or "why" questions or a student in the Intermediate Fluency stage being asked to perform a Preproduction-stage task, such as pointing to an object.

The so-called "Ramirez Report" (Ramirez, 1992) found that in all the language programs studied, including immersion as well as early-exit and late-exit transitional bilingual education, teachers tended to ask low-level questions. By knowing the stages of language acquisition and the stage-appropriate questions, you can engage students at the correct level of discourse. In addition, when appropriate questions are asked, content knowledge can be assessed alongside language proficiency.

Knowing the level of language acquisition also allows you to work within the student's "zone of proximal development"—that area between what the student is capable of at the moment and the point you want the student to reach next (Vygotsky, 1978). According to Vygotsky, you can work in a student's zone of proximal development by "scaffolding" language development, or providing the support a student needs as she progresses.

Scaffolding is essentially a way to nudge a student toward a higher level of performance. With language development, this can be done by modeling correct grammar or pronunciation, asking challenging questions, or providing direct instruction. For example, if a student is in the Preproduction stage, he will be successful at stage-appropriate tasks such as pointing, finding, or circling a picture. However, you can scaffold further development by supporting him as he attempts tasks characteristic of the Early Production stage, such as answering yes/no or either/or questions or providing one-word responses.

Recognizing the level of language acquisition is also a factor when setting language objectives. This can best be explained by Krashen's input hypothesis ($i + 1$), which builds upon the scaffolding approach described above (i = actual level and $i + 1$ = potential level of language development; Krashen & Terrell, 1983). Krashen's hypothesis states that a speaker will move to the next level of acquisition when the experience of the target language (the input) includes some of the structures that are part of the next stage of acquisition, and the speaker is encouraged to use language that reflects that more advanced stage.

Paying attention to teacher prompts that accompany the levels is one way for a student to move to the next level of English proficiency. If you adapt the way you prompt, students will respond according to both their current stage and the stage just beyond.

A common question teachers ask is, "How long does it take an English language learner to pass through the stages of language acquisition so that he can perform as well as a native English speaker in school?" In answer to this question, let's take a look at Figure 2.2.

Picture the English language as an iceberg divided into two parts: conversational language and academic language. The tip of the

Figure 2.2
Surface and Deeper Level of Language Proficiency

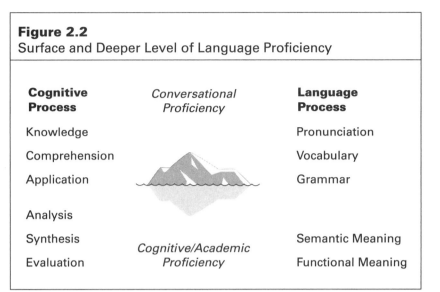

Cognitive Process	Conversational Proficiency	Language Process
Knowledge		Pronunciation
Comprehension		Vocabulary
Application		Grammar
Analysis		
Synthesis	Cognitive/Academic Proficiency	Semantic Meaning
Evaluation		Functional Meaning

Source: Cummins, James. *Bilingualism and special education: Issues in assessment and pedagogy.* Clevedon, England: Multilingual Matters. Copyright 1984. Reprinted by permission of the author.

iceberg—the small part that is visible above water—is conversational English, or basic interpersonal communicative skills. This is the language of normal everyday speech, including pronunciation, grammar, and basic vocabulary. It is the ability to understand and speak informally with friends, teachers, and parents. This conversational ability is not especially demanding intellectually. It is the language that non-English-speaking children develop after about two years of living in an English-speaking country.

Because they have developed a conversational ability, these children sound fluent to many people. They understand the teacher's questions, converse with classmates in English, and even translate for their parents. However, their daily schoolwork and exams may not reflect this fluency. Frustrated parents and teachers, faced with this contradiction, often conclude falsely that such students have learning disabilities, are poorly motivated, or are just plain lazy.

Let's go back to the iceberg. If we apply the iceberg metaphor to our fluent but underachieving students, we are likely to see that they have only developed the tip (i.e., conversational English). They have not developed academic English—the large portion of the iceberg that is hidden under the sea.

Academic English, or cognitive academic language proficiency, is the language of the classroom—the language of isosceles triangles, complex compound sentences, and photosynthesis. Students must master academic English to understand textbooks, write papers and reports, solve mathematical word problems, and take tests. Without a mastery of academic English, students cannot develop the critical-thinking and problem-solving skills needed to understand and express the new and abstract concepts taught in the classroom. However, academic language takes at least five to seven years to develop, and it can take even longer for a student who was not literate in her primary language when she started in a U.S. school (Collier & Thomas, 1989).

In the chapters that follow, you will find examples of instructional strategies that have been modified to meet the needs of ELLs according to their language acquisition level. You will also find examples of how to engage these students in whole-class activities by asking tiered questions associated with their level of language acquisition. Each chapter features an example of how an instructional strategy can be adapted for Preproduction, Early Production, Speech Emergence, and Intermediate and Advanced Fluency students. By providing stage-appropriate adaptations of instructional strategies, we hope to help you achieve the greatest possible success with your ELLs.

Classroom Examples

Here are examples of the kinds of adaptations you will find in the following chapters.

Subject: Literacy
Content Objective: To help students learn the basics of summarization.

A 1st grade teacher is teaching students to summarize using a Big Book version of *The Three Little Pigs*. She can help her ELLs acquire a better understanding of summarizing by using tiered questions in different ways depending on the stage of the student.

Preproduction
Students can point to a picture in the book as the teacher says or asks: "Show me the wolf. Where is the house?"

Early Production
Students do well with yes/no questions and one- or two-word answers: "Did the brick house fall down? Who blew down the straw house?"

Speech Emergence
Students can answer "why" and "how" questions with phrases or short-sentence answers, and can also explain their answers: "Explain why the third pig built his house out of bricks."

Intermediate Fluency
Students can answer "What would happen if" and "Why do you think" questions: "Why do you think the pigs were able to outsmart the wolf?"

Advanced Fluency
Students can retell the story, including the main plot elements and leaving out the insignificant details.

In addition to using tiered questions to include all students in a whole-class activity, you can also use these questioning strategies one-on-one with ELLs to check for comprehension.

The Word-MES Strategy

The Word-MES formula is another strategy you can use to enhance language development. Jane Hill, one of the authors of this book, named this formula based on her experiences learning to speak Spanish in Mexico and Spain. She knew what she wanted to say, but when she tried to say it she ended up in a big word mess—entangled in an utterance of disjointed nouns, verbs, and adjectives. Today, when she works with ELLs on language development, she uses the phrase "Word-MES" to remind her to

1. Work on **word** selection with Preproduction students,
2. **M**odel for Early Production students,
3. **E**xpand what Speech Emergence students have said or written, and
4. Help Intermediate and Advanced Fluency students "**s**ound like a book."

Here is how the 1st grade teacher in our classroom example can employ the Word-MES formula with ELLs at different stages.

Preproduction
Students need help with word selection. They need to learn vocabulary words such as "wolf," "pig," "house," "straw," "bricks," and "blow."

Early Production
Students benefit from you modeling good English. If a student says, "Wolf blowed," you can say, "Yes, the wolf blew and blew." Note that explicit corrections should not be made.

Speech Emergence
Students should focus on expanding oral and written sentences. If a student says, "He blew the house down," you can say, "Yes, he blew the straw house down." You have expanded by adding an adjective.

Intermediate and Advanced Fluency

Students should sound like a book. You can help them achieve this by exposing them to words beyond their current repertoire.

Furthermore, in the early grades, students acquire vocabulary through repeated readings of the same book or singing the same chants and familiar songs over and over. Word walls are a way for all ELLs to increase word knowledge while engaged in such activity. See Figure 2.3 for a word wall based on *The Little Red Hen*.

Summary

When you are familiar with the stages of second language acquisition, you will be more attuned to the appropriate types of questions and prompts to use to engage and motivate your ELLs. By understanding your students' levels of linguistic proficiency, you will become more competent at differentiating instruction to promote linguistic and academic achievement. You will also feel better, because students will participate and feel more confident as they successfully respond.

Figure 2.3
Word Wall

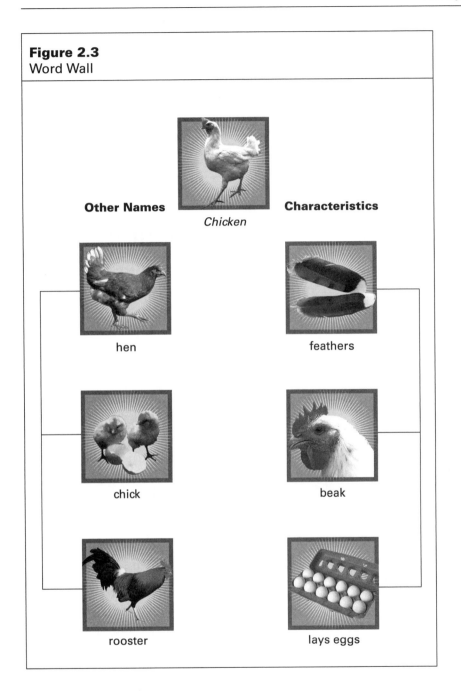

Other Names

Chicken

Characteristics

hen

feathers

chick

beak

rooster

lays eggs

3

SETTING OBJECTIVES AND PROVIDING FEEDBACK

Setting objectives in the classroom helps focus the direction for learning and establish the path for teaching. For ELLs, setting objectives is especially important: Imagine the incredible amount of incoming stimuli bombarding these students as they try to learn both a new language *and* content knowledge. This sense of being overwhelmed can subside when students are told exactly what they are going to learn each day upon entering the classroom. Aware of the intended outcomes, they now know what to focus on and what to screen out as they process new information.

The educational environment also becomes a friendlier place for ELLs when they have a clearly stated target for learning. When you set objectives correctly, students work toward clearly defined goals and are able to explain what they are learning and why they are learning it.

It is critical to set both content objectives and language objectives for ELLs. Just as language learning cannot occur if we only focus on subject matter, content knowledge cannot grow if we only focus on learning the English language.

The No Child Left Behind Act (NCLB) requires evidence of progress in both academic achievement and English language proficiency for ELLs. Researchers and educators have strongly supported the integration of content and language objectives (Chamot & O'Malley, 1994; Crandall, Spanos, Christian, Simich-Dudgeon, & Willetts, 1987; Dong, 2004/2005; Genesee, 1994; Mohan, 1990; Short, 1991; Simich-Dudgeon, McCreedy, & Schleppegrell, 1988). Systematic language development has to take place for students to eventually have the academic literacy skills they need to survive in the classroom. A firm foundation in academic English skills is necessary in order to meet content standards and pass challenging state assessments. Yet the question remains: How can we, as teachers, develop the language proficiency of ELLs while at the same time delivering content instruction?

Brinton, Snow, and Wesche (1989) offer four reasons for combining language objectives with content objectives:

1. **Language forms and vocabulary will develop as students study areas of interest.** Correct grammatical form and necessary vocabulary are best learned in the context of content areas (e.g., modeling the past tense when talking about history).
2. **Motivation plays a role in learning complex language structures.** Low motivation can hinder language acquisition because, as with low self-esteem and anxiety, it blocks language stimulation from reaching the brain. This block is also known as an "affective filter" (Krashen & Terrell, 1983). High motivation, on the other hand, results in an increased ability to learn and use a new language.
3. **Teachers can activate and build on students' prior knowledge in the content area.** ELLs may not have studied the American Revolution in their native country, but they may have studied another revolution or even experienced a modern conflict in their homeland. By accessing and activating such knowledge, you can prepare students to learn about analogous events in U.S. history.
4. **Language structure and form should be learned in authentic contexts rather than through contrived drills in language workbooks.** For example, when studying the American Revolution, students may learn about the type of clothing relevant to the 18th century. You can initiate the use of if-then statements by asking the class, "If you had to wear a uniform, how would you show your individuality?" While English-dominant students can write their ideas, ELLs can verbalize their thoughts using the sentence starter: "If I had to wear a uniform, then I would . . . ."

Educators started using such content-based ESL instruction—also called sheltered instruction—in the 1980s. The use of the phrases "content-based ESL" and "sheltered instruction" varies based on geography (Ovando, Collier, & Combs, 2003). In the eastern half of the United States, the labels "ESL content" and "content ESL" are used, whereas those on the West Coast tend to use "sheltered instruction." In California, the phrase used is "specially designed academic instruction in English," or SDAIE. We will use "sheltered instruction" in this book.

Sheltered instruction has long been the medium for delivering content knowledge in a way that allows both concepts and academic English proficiency to be nourished. In sheltered instruction, academic content is taught to ELLs in English by using techniques such as speaking slowly, using visual aids and manipulatives, and avoiding the use of idioms. Devices and procedures for sheltering instruction include the following:

- Manipulatives, miniature objects, realia
- Visuals (photos, pictures, drawings)
- Body movement and pantomime
- Facial expressions and gestures
- Clear expression and articulation
- Short, simple sentences
- Eye contact with students
- High-frequency vocabulary
- Reduction of idiomatic expressions
- Personalized language and nouns favored over pronouns
- More description through synonyms
- Prior content introduction (preview)

The Sheltered Instruction Observation Protocol (SIOP), developed by Echevarria, Vogt, and Short (2000), is a research-based model that many mainstream teachers use to better instruct ELLs. This model meets the NCLB requirement that a school's method of language instruction be research-based. The SIOP was first used as a research instrument; its effectiveness was tested over six years by the National Center for Research on Education, Diversity and Excellence before it was modified into a system for lesson planning and instruction. It emphasizes both content and language objectives in grade-level curriculum, helping teachers and schools teach English to ELLs while also helping students meet challenging state standards.

The SIOP model makes academic content comprehensible and encourages language learning by highlighting key features of the English language. To do this effectively, teachers must set content objectives while also reviewing which linguistic functions and structures in the lesson students will need in order to effectively participate.

Determining Language Functions and Structures

Fathman, Quinn, and Kessler (1992) point out that "language functions are specific uses of language for accomplishing certain purposes" (p. 12). (A lesson using similarities and differences, for example, would have the language function of comparing.) Let's suppose you are working with a 2nd grade class on communities. You ask the students to make a map of the community and provide directions from home to school, or from school to a nearby park. What function of language will the students need to complete this exercise? The language function (or purpose) required in this instance is giving directions. Are there other English demands in this lesson? Are certain language structures, such as particular verb tenses, possessives, plurals, adverbs, or vocabulary words, needed to communicate the directions from home to school or to the park? When you take these issues into consideration, you will see that students need to know the command form of the verb "to go" and also be well versed in numbers and directional vocabulary (i.e., "Go two blocks and turn right") in order to successfully complete the assignment.

According to Gibbons (1991), a multitude of language functions occur in the classroom each day, including the following:

- Agreeing and disagreeing
- Apologizing
- Asking for assistance or directions
- Asking for permission
- Classifying
- Commanding/giving instructions
- Comparing
- Criticizing
- Denying
- Describing
- Enquiring/questioning
- Evaluating
- Explaining
- Expressing likes and dislikes
- Expressing obligation
- Expressing position
- Hypothesizing
- Identifying
- Inferring
- Planning and predicting
- Refusing
- Reporting
- Sequencing
- Suggesting
- Warning
- Wishing and hoping

Classroom Examples

Here are some examples from 6th grade mainstream teachers of how to determine the language functions and structures that need to be addressed in a lesson.

Example 1

Subject: Social Studies

Content Objective: To understand the period of the 1920s and the women's rights movement.

The language objective is determined by deciding on the function that language will have in the lesson, and by thinking about what language structures an ELL will need in order to participate in the lesson. Because students will be comparing what women *could* and *couldn't* do—and what they *did* and *didn't* do—in the 1920s, they will need the language function of comparing. The language structure is contractions. The language objective will be to learn contractions in order to make comparisons.

Example 2

Subject: Science

Content Objective: To understand the sequential pattern of an experiment and how one step affects another.

In this lesson, explaining the steps of a science experiment is the needed language function. Because if-then statements are a type of language structure we use to explain sequence in English, the language objective is to use if-then statements to explain the steps of the experiment. If necessary, you can model sentences for students (e.g., "If the temperature of the solution changes, then viscosity . . .").

Example 3

Subject: Math

Content Objective: To comprehend the differences between two or more polygons.

The needed language function is classifying. Because students will need to understand comparative structures such as "greater than" and "less than," the language objective becomes using "greater than," "less than," "similar," and "equal to" in classifying polygons.

Example 4

Subject: Language Arts

Content Objective: To learn how to express persuasive opinions.

The language function is persuading because the lesson involves forming opinions in order to be able to persuade. The language structure will be using the sentence starters "I think" and "In my opinion."

The language objective becomes using these sentence starters to express opinions.

Identifying Vocabulary and Key Concepts

Another way to set language objectives is to identify the vocabulary and key concepts of the lesson. Vocabulary instruction has been the subject of several recent books (Beck, McKeown, & Kucan, 2002; Marzano, 2004; Paynter, Bodrova, & Doty, 2005), all of which emphasize the importance of teaching vocabulary in relation to reading comprehension. Even though ELLs are taught vocabulary as soon as they enter U.S. classrooms, they still lag significantly behind their English-speaking peers. McLaughlin and colleagues (2000) report that over time, an enriched vocabulary program can close the gap in vocabulary knowledge and reading comprehension between ELLs and English-dominant students.

In the enriched vocabulary program that McLaughlin and colleagues cite, 12 vocabulary words were selected from short reading passages each week. Learning processes included discovering cognates, using strategies for inferring meaning from text, finding root words, participating in activities outside the classroom to deepen word meanings, and various other measures to enhance vocabulary growth and development. In a more recent study of direct vocabulary instruction with ELLs, strategies involving word analysis and instruction of essential vocabulary improved comprehension (Carlo et al., 2004).

Generalizations from *Classroom Instruction That Works*

Three generalizations on setting objectives can be drawn from the research in *Classroom Instruction That Works*.

1. Setting goals for instruction helps students focus attention on information specifically related to the goals.

2. Teachers should encourage students to personalize the learning goals identified for them. Once instructional goals are established, students should be urged to adapt them to personal needs and desires. ELLs can be encouraged to do so by using sentence starters such as "I want to know . . ." or "I wonder if . . . ."

3. Goals should not be too specific, as this will limit learning. A narrow learning goal (e.g., "Given five practice sessions, students will be able to connect 10 pictures with their matching vocabulary terms with 80 percent accuracy") will restrict the breadth of learning for ELLs. They will do better with a more general goal, such as "Students will be able to predict meanings of weather vocabulary by drawing pictures."

Classroom Recommendations

Based on the three generalizations above, *Classroom Instruction That Works* presents two recommendations for classroom practices: Set goals that are specific but flexible, and contract with students to attain specific learning goals.

The first recommendation parallels the third generalization above: Goals, though important, should be general enough to allow for some flexibility. The second recommendation—contracting with students to attain specific goals—helps ELLs because it gives them a great deal of control over their learning. For example, let's say the children in a kindergarten class decide at the beginning of each week how many "squares" they will earn. They earn squares for listening, helping, putting things away, and other behaviors. Each child fills out a contract by writing down his name and how many squares he plans to earn. The teacher notes the squares on a clipboard, and at the end of the week, she reconciles the accomplishments with the contracts. Those who meet the contract agreements earn token rewards, such as bookmarks or pencils.

Classroom Example

Here is an example from a 3rd grade classroom that shows how you can take a lesson designed for English-speaking students and modify it to set language objectives for ELLs in each stage of language acquisition.

Subject: Social Studies
Content Objective: To help students understand that making choices can be difficult because it often involves trade-offs.

Because money is a limited resource, people must make important choices about how to spend it. These choices often involve trade-offs: People must often give up buying one thing in order to buy something else. To help students understand the concept of trade-offs, ask students to imagine that they are going on a camping trip and have $120 they have saved to spend on camping supplies.

The local camping supply store offers certain types of supplies at the specified prices (see Figure 3.1). Ask students: "Which supplies will you buy, and why? Which will you choose to go without, and why?" Tell students that they will need to make a list of the supplies they will buy, the prices for each item, the total amount they will spend, and the reasons they have made these particular choices.

Figure 3.1
Prices of Supplies for "Going Camping" Activity

Backpack: $40	Flashlight: $8
Binoculars: $30	Lightweight radio: $30
Canteen: $6	Matches: $3
Compass: $10	Rain poncho: $5
Cooking set: $30	Sewing kit: $3
Emergency blanket: $15	Six-inch hunting knife: $12
Emergency candle: $7	Swiss army knife: $25
Emergency supply kit: $25	Tent for two people: $35
Emergency towel: $3	Tent for three people: $60
Fire-starter kit: $7	Utensils: $3

When students have completed the activity, initiate a class discussion about the choices that they made. Which items were most commonly chosen by the students? Which items were the least popular choices? What were the factors that influenced the students' decisions in making trade-offs?

Preproduction

The language objective is to learn the vocabulary of camping supplies, the language function is naming, and the language structure is vocabulary words. While the English-dominant students are working on the activity, Preproduction students can work in a small group with you. They could learn the words necessary for this lesson, which should include all the items, along with the prices. You will need the items, or at least pictures of them. After learning the vocabulary, the students could be given play money and allowed to buy certain items.

Steps for teaching vocabulary at this stage are as follows:

1. Identify a new word and elicit background knowledge. You can do this by showing several pictures and prompting

students to identify them by asking questions (e.g., "Which one is the flashlight?").

2. Explain the meaning of the word with pictures and gestures.
3. Have students create a visual representation of the new word.

Early Production

The language objective is to use the vocabulary of camping supplies and correct grammar, the language function is naming and labeling, and the language structure is grammatical components. Early Production students can match the camping items or pictures to the written words. They can also put price tags on items. Students at this stage can be given play money and allowed to buy certain items. If you give them a limited amount of money, they will have to make some choices.

You should circulate during this activity. When you confer with students, you will hear grammatical errors. Students should never be overtly corrected, but it is always appropriate to model back correct English usage. For example, if a student says, "Buy tent," you model by saying: "Oh, you want to buy the tent."

Speech Emergence

The language objective is to speak and write expanded sentences using "because," the language function is explaining and describing, and the language structure is "because." Some Speech Emergence students may be able to complete the objective as stated for English-dominant students. The students may need to review the items and the vocabulary associated with the items. This could be done either with you or with English-dominant students in the class.

These students will need assistance putting together an answer for your question: "Which supplies will you choose to go without, and why?" You might give them some sentence starters that encourage verbal or written use of "because." For example: "I'm not going to buy (item name) because . . ." or "Because (item name) is (price), I'm going to buy it."

Intermediate and Advanced Fluency

The language objective is to participate in a class discussion by agreeing with factors already heard or by introducing new factors, the language function is discussing the factors that influenced trade-offs, and the language structure is expressing influencing factors during discussion. (In a discussion, a student can add on to what another student says or introduce a new idea.)

Intermediate and Advanced Fluency students can participate in the activity as designed for mainstream students. You will hear fewer and fewer grammatical errors. Students' decisions will be influenced by their own opinions; there are no right or wrong answers. During the whole-class discussion, you can introduce more academic vocabulary, which will help these students sound more like a book.

Feedback

Effective learning requires feedback. When teaching ELLs, it is particularly important to ensure that your feedback is comprehensible, useful, and relevant.

Oliver (2003) notes that the way in which teachers correct language usage affects students' verbal modifications. When teacher feedback on errors is constructive, students use the feedback to rephrase. According to Schoen and Schoen (2003) and Short (1991), rather than immediately correcting students, teachers should simply restate what the students say using the correct grammar, pronunciation, or vocabulary. Students can refer to this model in the future when they want to say something similar. Modeling correct grammar is beneficial for the student, but overemphasizing grammar is not.

To be able to give feedback on language, you must have a firm foundation in how our language works. Wong Fillmore and Snow (2000) put forth a strong rationale for the need for classroom teachers to understand language function and structure: Because knowledge of English language usage has been emphasized less and less over time, they recommend more training for teachers in the areas of linguistics, sociolinguistics, and language use.

Thornbury (1999) and Brown (2000) contend that if language learners only get positive messages about their output, they will not make attempts to restructure their grammar. If they think that everything they are saying is accurate, they will stop short of full language proficiency and their incorrect usage will become "fossilized." As an example, Thornbury recommends some possible responses for teachers when responding to the error in the sentence "He has a long hair":

- "*He has long hair.*" This is a correction in the strictest sense of the word. The teacher simply repairs the student's utterance.
- "*No article.*" The teacher's move is directed at pinpointing the kind of error the student has made in order to prompt self-correction.
- "*I'm sorry, I didn't understand.*" This is known as a clarification request.
- "*A long hair is just one single hair, like you find in your soup. For the hair on your head you wouldn't use an article; you would say:*

He has long hair." This is an example of reactive teaching, where instruction is in response to errors.

- *"Oh, he has long hair, has he?"* This technique (sometimes called reformulation) is an example of covert feedback, disguised as a conversational aside.

Error correction can take many forms; it varies from the simple to the complex. Talk with your school's ESL teachers regarding the forms of error correction that work best for them. In this book, we will be reminding you to model by repairing (first example above) and reformulating (last example above) when an ELL makes an error.

Generalizations from *Classroom Instruction That Works*

The authors of *Classroom Instruction That Works* gleaned four generalizations about feedback from the research.

1. Feedback should be corrective in nature. The more information you can provide on what is correct and what is incorrect about a student's oral or written responses, the better. This can be helpful to ELLs, but not when correcting their grammatical errors or their articulation mistakes. As discussed above, the best way to provide corrective feedback when grammar or pronunciation errors are made is simply to model the correct English without overtly calling attention to the error.

2. Feedback should be timely. Timing can be critical for ELLs, particularly when you are offering feedback by verbally modeling correct grammar or pronunciation.

3. Feedback should be criterion-referenced. The research indicates that using criterion-referenced feedback is better than using norm-referenced feedback. In other words, telling students how they are progressing in learning specific types of knowledge and skills is better than giving them a score reflecting the number of correct answers. The practice of using rubrics, a method of providing criterion-referenced feedback, is especially helpful for ELLs.

4. Students can effectively provide some of their own feedback through self-evaluation. ELLs can monitor their own progress in learning English and subject matter by keeping track of their performance as language and academic learning occurs.

Classroom Recommendations

We recommend using rubrics to provide feedback on declarative knowledge (information) or procedural knowledge (processes and skills). This practice produces many benefits when used with ELLs in a mainstream class. When rubrics are tied to a student's work, the student better understands expectations. Rubrics also allow grading to be less subjective and more comprehensible to the student.

If ELLs can be involved in the development of their own rubrics, all the better! When rubrics are jointly constructed, there is a clearer understanding of what constitutes an acceptable performance, and the rubric score becomes far more meaningful than a traditional letter grade or even a teacher-created rubric.

Teachers should also be sure to provide feedback on assessments. Some of the best feedback you can give ELLs is letting them know what was correct or incorrect in their use of written English. You will need to walk a careful line when correcting errors, as you want to identify essential corrections but not overwhelm or discourage students by identifying *all* of the errors you see or hear.

When giving feedback on written language, you should make sure that students understand a system of correction symbols, such as those presented in Figure 3.2.

Figure 3.2
Correction Symbols

Symbol	Meaning
^	*Insert*
¶	*New paragraph*
≡	*Capitalize*
V.T.	*Verb tense*
A.N.	*Adjective–noun order*
Subj.	*Need subject*

As a student's English proficiency progresses, errors can be marked in ways that require more and more of the student's attention. Earle-Carline (n.d.) recommends the following approach to marking errors for ELLs, in which the teacher scaffolds learning by making the student work harder to identify the error as her English proficiency increases:

1. Circle or underline each error and write the correction symbol above it.
2. Highlight the error without supplying the symbol.
3. Write only the symbol in the margin of any line with this error.
4. Put only a check in the margin indicating that there is an error of some sort. (p. 1)

Classroom Instruction That Works also recommends student-led feedback, in which students explain to each other—in pairs or small groups—what is correct or incorrect in a product. However, peer feedback never means that students score each other's papers or issue grades to each other. Fathman and colleagues (1992) report that, for ELLs, peer feedback can be more beneficial than teacher feedback because the students may feel less self-conscious receiving corrections or recommendations in a small group.

The Word-MES formula can help you to match oral and written corrective feedback to your ELLs' stage of language acquisition as follows.

Preproduction

Students will benefit from help with vocabulary and word selection. These students can respond by pointing or gesturing. Instead of asking a question requiring a verbal response, prompt with "Point to" or "Show me." After students point, give feedback by saying, "Yes, that is a (name of item)."

Early Production

Students need you to provide feedback by modeling correct English whenever possible. For example, if a student says or writes, "Goed the game," model the correct utterance by offering, "Oh, you went to the game." The key here is subtle modeling. Overt correction can inhibit a student from using language.

"Syntax surgery" is a useful strategy for helping students to see differences between the word order in English and the word order in their primary language (Herrell & Jordan, 2004). First, you identify a sentence the student has said or written incorrectly. Then you write the words on a sentence strip, cut it apart, and reorganize the words into correct English order. When students see the sentence rearrangement and hear your explanation, they are more likely to use the correct syntax in the future. For example, placing the adjective after the noun is a common mistake for Spanish-speaking students when learning English, as this is the correct word order in Spanish. To perform syntax surgery, you would select a phrase or sentence (e.g., "dog brown") and rearrange it in the correct order ("brown dog") while explaining why you did so.

Speech Emergence

Students can use your assistance focusing on finer points of grammar by expanding a sentence verbally or by writing an expanded sentence for the student. If the student says or writes, "The boy wore a coat to school," the teacher can expand the sentence by adding an adjective: "The boy wore a warm coat to school." A student in this stage could also be exposed to using coordinating conjunctions (e.g., *and, but, or*) in compound sentences. You can therefore expand what these students say or write by joining two simple sentences.

Intermediate and Advanced Fluency

Students should be using language to compare, describe, debate, persuade, justify, create, and evaluate so they can sound like a book. The structure of their sentences, the use of vocabulary, and the overall organization of their written work should be approximating the writing of their English-speaking peers. Thus, you can provide feedback that is similar to the kind you would offer native English speakers. It is important for these students to be exposed to a more sophisticated form of language.

Summary

Setting clear language and content objectives for ELLs is critical for effective teaching and learning. English language learners have to learn not only the content of a subject but also the language of a subject. Stimulating English through word selection (vocabulary), modeling, expanding, and helping students sound more like a book can make subject learning and language learning happen simultaneously. Students are doing double duty by learning a new language and new information, just as you are doing double duty by identifying content objectives and sources for language objectives.

Two things ELLs really want to know are "Will the teacher like me?" and "Can I do the work?" Providing feedback on English acquisition will demonstrate a level of "like" they may not have experienced before. Errors are going to naturally occur in the process of learning a second language, and the best way for you, as a teacher, to deal with them is to model correct structures by unceremoniously restating what students say. Overtly correcting grammar and pronunciation can generate anxiety, which in turn can inhibit natural language acquisition.

4

NONLINGUISTIC REPRESENTATIONS

Knowledge is stored in two ways: linguistically and nonlinguistically. Teachers mainly present new knowledge linguistically in the classroom, as they often ask students to listen to or read new information. Think of knowledge presented linguistically as actual sentences stored in long-term memory. Knowledge that is presented nonlinguistically is stored in the form of mental pictures or physical sensations such as sight, sound, smell, touch, taste, and movement. Using both linguistic and nonlinguistic methods of learning helps students recall and think about information. Because ELLs cannot rely solely on linguistic ability to learn and retain knowledge in a new language, nonlinguistic methods of learning are particularly important for them.

Using modes other than the English language to communicate has long been a mainstay in the tool kit of ESL teachers. To make English instruction as understandable as possible for ELLs, Short (1991) recommends using diverse media, including realia (real objects), graphs, photos, maps, and demonstrations. Short makes these suggestions for mainstream teachers (1991, p. 8):

- **Bring realia into the lessons.** Nonverbal information can be communicated by using real objects and visuals such as photographs, graphs, and charts.

- **Conduct demonstrations.** Match actions with your words to convey meaning. Give directions by pointing, gesturing, showing, and explaining.
- **Use filmstrips, films, videotapes, and audiocassettes with books.** Words alone on a page will not hold meaning for students in the early stages of language acquisition. Students can connect with content better when they see *and* hear it.
- **Have the students do hands-on activities.** Conducting science experiments, performing pantomime, drawing pictures, and sequencing stories are all useful hands-on activities.

Meaning cannot be conveyed to ELLs through words alone. Their instruction must be supplemented with real objects, visuals, body language, facial expressions, gestures, and hands-on experiences.

Generalizations from *Classroom Instruction That Works*

Two generalizations about nonlinguistic representations can be drawn from *Classroom Instruction That Works*.

1. A variety of activities can help students to formulate nonlinguistic representations. These strategies include the use of graphic representations, pictures, mental images, physical and technological models, and kinesthetic (movement) activities.

2. Nonlinguistic representations elaborate on knowledge. For example, ELLs can add to their knowledge when asked to construct a mental model of a fraction in concrete form (e.g., a pizza sliced in different quantities). Further elaboration takes place when the student explains how the model represents fractions. Preproduction and Early Production students will do better with constructing a physical representation than with explaining it in spoken or written language. Students in the other, higher stages of language acquisition should be able to construct a model as well as to verbally explain it.

Classroom Recommendations

Classroom Instruction That Works offers five recommendations for using nonlinguistic representations in the classroom.

1. Use graphic organizers to represent knowledge. Graphic organizers, which include Venn diagrams, charts, webs, and time lines, can be designed to make complex content more understandable for ELLs. Textbooks can often be too complicated for these students. Graphic organizers help them understand knowledge and store it in another way. There are five commonly used types of graphic organizers (see Appendix A): vocabulary terms and phrases, time sequence, cause/effect sequence, episodes, and generalizations/principles.

Do not, however, automatically assume that your students know how to use graphic organizers. A study by Tang (1994) found that intermediate social studies textbooks in Hong Kong, Japan, and Mexico contain few graphic organizers, meaning you will need to model their use for ELLs from those countries and possibly others.

2. Use symbolic representations, such as pictures, pictographs, maps, and diagrams. In order for ELLs to understand text, they must make connections between what they already know and the new information presented. As they make these connections, they construct meaning and begin to comprehend the material. Figures 4.1 and 4.2 are examples of pictographs, which help students visualize information, recognize patterns, and remember new content, such as vocabulary.

Because ELLs enter the U.S. school system with background knowledge in their primary language, pictures and pictographs related to this knowledge can help bridge the language gap. (Tang's 1994 study found that most of the illustrations in Chinese, Japanese, and Mexican intermediate social studies textbooks were representational pictures—common, everyday photographs and drawings of how things look.)

3. Teachers should help students generate mental pictures. When ELLs listen or read, creating a "movie in the mind" helps them to understand and store knowledge. Using all five senses can help produce rich mental images. For example, when studying the Ming dynasty, a teacher asked her class to close their eyes and relate what they heard when she said the words "Ming dynasty." Responses included "Ping" and "Chinese music." Next, the teacher asked what they smelled. Students described such aromas as "old and mildewy," "musty," and "Chinese food." When asked what they felt, student responses included "cold like a vase" and "spicy." Finally, when the teacher asked what they saw, the students produced many images, including "an antique vase" and "an emperor in a beautiful robe."

We do current events each morning—that's an Arizona state standard for public speaking. Two or three students a day need to present their current event. The students who are listening draw their nonlinguistic representations, either on the subject of the event or [of two or three] specific vocabulary [words] that I'll write on the chalkboard. . . . The students either draw a picture or engage in an artistic endeavor.

—*William Gibson,*
Kayenta Intermediate School,
Kayenta, Arizona

Figure 4.1
Pictograph Example

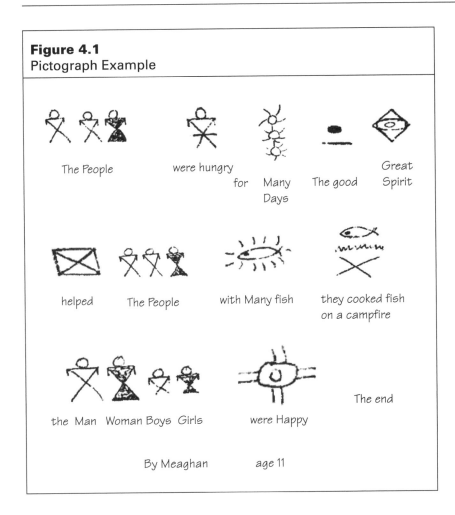

We do lots of pictures with our spelling words. With generating mental pictures, I ask [students] to close their eyes or put their heads down, and I ask them to picture what we are talking about or what they are going to do before they meet with their partners. They really learn best by doing it—by touching it, by acting it out. Especially in 2nd grade, those students who are in their first year in a U.S. school are bombarded with a million vocabulary words—not just the specific vocabulary that I pick out but also the social vocabulary, the academic vocabulary, and then the vocabulary we are setting aside for the students who already speak English. So, it's a lot to take in.

*—Lindsay Moses,
North Elementary School,
Brighton, Colorado*

4. Make physical models. Physical models are concrete representations of what is being learned. When students use manipulatives, they are making a physical model to represent knowledge. Manipulatives are commonly associated with math (e.g., shapes, cubes, money) but can actually be incorporated in all content areas through such items as puzzles, maps, word sorts, and Legos. For example, instead of labeling the 50 states, assembling a puzzle made up of pieces representing each state would be a good way to use a physical model during a geography lesson.

Any three-dimensional form can be a physical model. For ELLs, the very act of constructing a concrete representation establishes an "image" of the knowledge, so they do not have to depend solely on words.

5. Engage students in kinesthetic activities in which they represent knowledge using physical movement. Total Physical Response (TPR) has been a popular ESL approach over the years. Developed by

I use mental pictures. I have [students] draw out what they think it might be or create a picture in their head. For example, we were talking today about the rain forest, so one of the girls came up and said, "I have a mental picture of Miss Hitchcock wearing brown shorts and a vest and safari hat. I see her in the jungle." I think these mental pictures help a lot because [students] can refer back to that image.

—*Denise Hitchcock,*
North Elementary School,
Brighton, Colorado

We do the movement thing, too. If somebody were to come in who doesn't really know anything about teaching, they would think some of the things we do are really dorky. For example, when we are studying condensation and precipitation, we all dance around the room—we are clouds, and it's raining. If somebody else were to walk in, they would think, "This is not education. Why are the kids dancing?" And when they are doing the grids, learning how to do the x-axis first, then we always make the letter L using their index finger and thumb. You will see them taking their math test and holding up a hand with index finger and thumb in the L position.

—*Elisabeth Berry,*
North Elementary School,
Brighton, Colorado

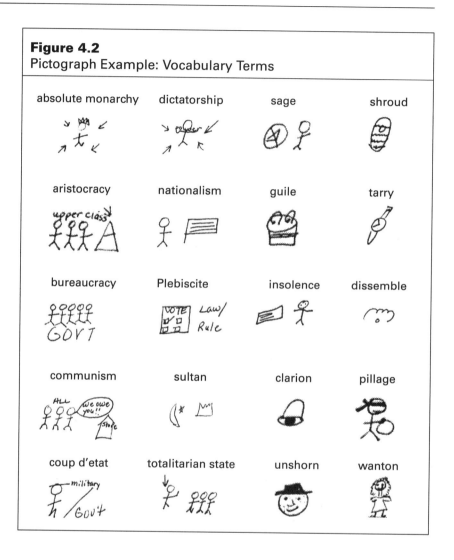

Figure 4.2
Pictograph Example: Vocabulary Terms

James Asher (1977), TPR uses kinesthetic activities to teach English. Students engage in active language learning by demonstrating their comprehension through body movements. In early lessons, students are directed to stand up, turn around, sit down, or clap their hands. More complex commands follow, with participants eventually verbalizing commands to the instructor and their classmates.

Berty Segal popularized the TPR approach in his book *Teaching English Through Action* (1983). Based on the framework of normal first language development, Segal's methodology centered on the belief that reading and writing skills would be acquired after a firm foundation in listening and speaking was established. Students enjoy the gamelike qualities of TPR and value the opportunity to develop their listening skills before being required to verbally produce the new language.

Kinesthetic activities can also be used to improve content knowledge. How do you think a Preproduction student will most easily understand a lesson on how an electric circuit works: by hearing a lecture, reading a text, or acting it out? Would students at other stages of language development also benefit from acting things out (the planets rotating around the sun, for example)? Geometry is another content area where kinesthetic activities work well: ELLs will have a greater chance of learning and recalling terms if they use their arms to represent the radius, diameter, and circumference of circles or the right, acute, and obtuse angles of polygons. In history, drama, or English language arts, acting out an event or a story helps generate a mental image of the knowledge in the mind of the learner.

Classroom Example

Below is an example of how you can use a graphic organizer with ELLs.

Subject: Science
Content Objective: To classify organisms based on physical characteristics.
  The class reads the following passage:

> What are the main characteristics of reptiles?
>   A **reptile** (rep´tīl) is a cold-blooded vertebrate that has lungs and dry skin. Almost all reptiles have scales. Most reptiles live on land and lay eggs. Some give birth to live young. The eggs of reptiles are laid on land. These eggs have a tough covering that prevents the eggs from drying out on land. There are four main groups of reptiles. These are the alligators and crocodiles, the snakes, the lizards, and the turtles.

You can use the graphic organizer in Figure 4.3 to help students store knowledge about reptiles. Some of the circles can be left empty for a whole-class activity. The graphic organizer actually combines linguistic information (words and phrases) with nonlinguistic information (circles and lines representing relationships). It is called a descriptive pattern organizer because it represents facts that can be organized to describe characteristics of specific people, places, things, or events.

I definitely use a lot of visuals in my class to help make my second-language learners understand. I do a lot of vocabulary skits where students have to act out the meaning of a word.
—*Kelly Gardner,*
Berry Creek Middle School,
Edwards, Colorado

We do a lot of movement. Even if we are studying phonics and talking about phonics and talking about long and short sounds, I ask, "What are we going to do when we hear a long sound? What are we going to do when we hear a short sound?" Students move and make up the action. You will see them later in the year doing that same thing. Or with putting compound words together, they will start out with their hands apart, and then you see their hands come together—"Oh, dog house," (clap) "doghouse." It's that whole action thing.
—*D. H.*

Figure 4.3
Graphic Organizer for "Reptiles" Classroom Example

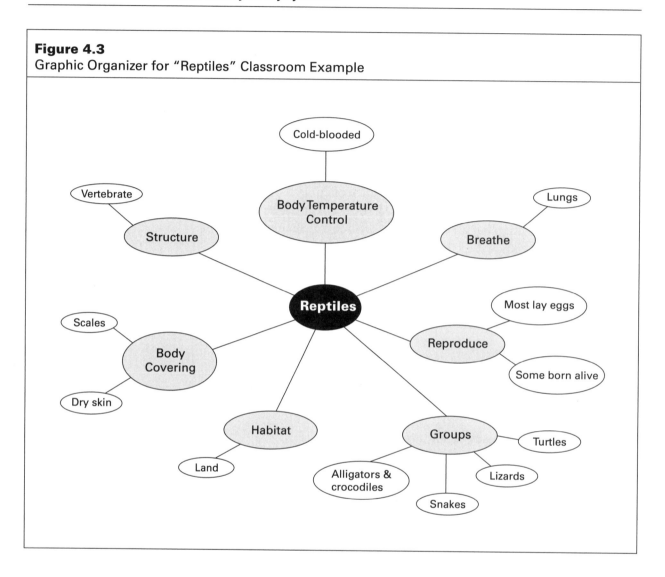

Preproduction
Students need to have pictures associated with the above topic and facts. During the class discussion, you can engage these students by using "Show me" or "Point to the" prompts.

Early Production
Students benefit from the pictures associated with reptiles and need to be encouraged to use the vocabulary. A cloze technique is effective in eliciting one-word responses. For example, you can lead students with phrases like: "A reptile breathes with . . ." or "The reptile's body is covered with . . . ."

Speech Emergence

Students will be able to comprehend the passage, particularly given the graphic organizer. They can answer questions requiring a phrase or short sentence, such as "Tell me about reptiles." Using questions that start with "Why" and "How" works well when eliciting responses at this level.

Intermediate and Advanced Fluency

Students will understand the passage and the graphic organizer, and can therefore be prompted with questions such as "How are they the same/different?" "What would happen if . . . ?" or "Why do you think . . . ?"

Once again, we remind you that anytime you use tiered questions, you should always take care to intermingle questions and prompts from your student's next stage of language acquisition in order to scaffold language development.

Summary

Lessons using nonlinguistic representations are highly appropriate instructional strategies for ELLs. Students at early stages of language acquisition—those without full command of essential vocabulary and English grammar—will have difficulty demonstrating their conceptual knowledge through writing or by taking a test that requires reading and writing. For this reason, it is important to allow your English language learners to demonstrate their understanding through nonlinguistic representations.

5

CUES, QUESTIONS, AND ADVANCE ORGANIZERS

Cues and Questions

Students construct meaning by drawing connections between new information and what they already know (background knowledge). Cues and questions are used at the beginning of a lesson to help students access and activate background knowledge and connect that knowledge to new learning. Background knowledge can consist of content knowledge, personal experiences, and certainly misconceptions.

Ovando and colleagues (2003) recognized the importance of prior knowledge in providing "rich clues to meaning" (p. 92). ELLs can use these clues to reach those "a-ha!" moments that come when they connect content presented in their new language with what they already know. Furthermore, in addition to revealing what students know about the subject matter, cues and questions help teachers discover what students need to know.

Building background is one of the eight components of the Sheltered Instruction Observation Protocol model discussed in Chapter 3 (Echevarria, Vogt, & Short, 2000). Teachers link new information to students' background knowledge by giving them cues—or hints—about what they are about to experience. For example, while watching a film about cats, a teacher can provide a cue by explaining that students will see some things they already know about cats and some things they do not know. By providing the topic of the film, the teacher has activated prior knowledge—the students will start thinking about what they already know about cats.

Questions can do the same thing—for example, the teacher could simply ask students what they know about cats. Questioning can take different forms. Simich-Dudgeon (1998) reports on three question–answer patterns:

1. **Question-response-evaluation.** The teacher asks a question and then appraises the answer.
2. **Question-response-feedback.** The teacher asks a question, the student answers, and then the teacher provides feedback. The teacher feedback takes the form of paraphrasing the student's answer, which leads to the student rephrasing his response.
3. **Student-organized interaction.** Students ask and answer questions in small groups. The teacher becomes a facilitator and discussion participant.

Although Simich-Dudgeon found question-response-feedback and student-organized interaction to have the most positive results with ELLs, you must always take into consideration a student's level of English proficiency when questioning. Tiered questions can be used with ELLs (see Chapter 2) precisely because they take into account the level of language acquisition, thus allowing students to be successful responders. To use tiered questions, you must monitor student communication and pose questions that allow students to participate with confidence and success.

You are encouraged to ask questions frequently throughout a lesson (Simich-Dudgeon, McCreedy, & Schleppegrell, 1988) because it provides many opportunities for ELLs to use their new language. Students will need a chance to put their thoughts into words, so providing some wait time after asking questions will lead to higher-quality responses. Participating in classroom interactions will help students gain confidence in themselves and their speaking abilities.

Teachers who ask tiered questions adjust their questions to maximize the ways in which the student can respond in the new language (Herrell & Jordan, 2004). After determining the stage of language acquisition, a teacher can decide if a student can be expected to point, use one- or two-word responses, answer with short phrases (some grammatical errors acceptable), or produce longer sentences (fewer grammatical errors acceptable). Questions can then be planned to elicit the desired level of response and ensure student involvement.

Wait time has been huge for me this year. This is the first year in an English classroom for one of my students. I think she understands quite a bit, but it takes her a long time to process and think. Plus, she's very shy and very quiet. I ask a question and wait because, given the opportunity, she wants to answer and she will figure out the answer. In small groups, I've noticed that the wait time is becoming less, and I think it's because she's more comfortable. She feels safer with her English in the small groups.

—E. B.

Generalizations from *Classroom Instruction That Works*

Classroom Instruction That Works provides four generalizations from the research when using cues and questions.

1. Cues and questions should focus on what is important rather than what is unusual. Teachers often structure cues or questions around something they perceive as interesting or unique, under the mistaken assumption that it will motivate students by piquing their interest. However, ELLs need to focus on what is important rather than on what is unusual, and they need to be able to filter out unnecessary information in order to grasp the critical content. For example, to introduce a unit on the solar system, a teacher might ask students what they know about UFOs. Although students might find this topic interesting, it does not activate any prior knowledge about the solar system. Having students—particularly ELLs—focus on superfluous material will take them off track, away from the primary learning objective.

2. Higher-level questions produce deeper learning than lower-level questions. Adapting questions for ELLs will be a new technique for many classroom teachers. You will need to understand the stages of language acquisition in order to appropriately adapt questions. See Chapter 2 for examples of how to use tiered questions with students at each level of language acquisition.

3. Waiting at least three seconds before accepting responses from students increases the depth of answers. A brief pause after asking a question is known as "wait time." When students are given more time to formulate their responses, they are likely to participate more in classroom discussions about the content. As noted earlier, wait time is particularly valuable for ELLs because it allows them time to think about not only what they are going to say, but also how they are going to say it in English.

4. Questions are effective even before a lesson begins. You may think that you should only ask questions after a learning experience. Research shows, however, that using questions before a learning experience can serve to activate and access prior knowledge.

Classroom Recommendations

Cues and questions need to be used before a lesson begins in order to activate background knowledge and to help students focus on what they will be learning. There are three recommendations from *Classroom Instruction That Works* for the use of cues and questions in the classroom.

1. Use explicit cues to access prior knowledge. Figure 5.1 depicts a K-W-L chart, which directly asks students what they already know about a topic.

Figure 5.1
K-W-L Chart

K (What I know)	W (What I want to learn)	L (What I learned)

English-dominant students as well as Speech Emergence, Intermediate, and Advanced Fluency learners can write about what they already know in a K-W-L format, while Preproduction and Early Production students can draw what they know. Use explicit cues to find out what students do and do not already know.

2. Ask questions that elicit inferences. Intermediate and Advanced Fluency students can make inferences in English, but Preproduction, Early Production, and Speech Emergence ELLs will have more difficulty because their levels of language acquisition limit their verbal and written output. To engage Preproduction students, ask questions that require a pointing or gesturing response. For Early Production students, ask yes/no questions, either/or questions, or questions requiring a one- or two-word response. Speech Emergence students can answer questions with a phrase or a short sentence.

A lot of times we will just start with the question, "What do you know about . . . ?" to access that background knowledge. Showing [students] a picture or physically bringing in something to show them will get them thinking about what we are going to be learning.

—*D. H.*

3. Use analytic questions. These types of questions will pose difficulties for students at early stages of language acquisition—not because the students do not possess the cognitive skills needed for analytical thinking but because of limits placed on their output by how far along they are in acquiring their second language. Therefore, you need to once again match the level of the question to the stage of language acquisition. Your skill at doing so will be challenged as you try to implement these recommendations. (You may wish to consult Figure 2.1 in Chapter 2, which depicts the stages of language acquisition along with appropriate teacher prompts for each stage.) You'll also want to keep Krashen's *i + 1* hypothesis and Vygotsky's zone of proximal development in mind when posing questions (again, see Chapter 2).

Advance Organizers

Advance organizers are organizational frameworks presented in advance of lessons that emphasize the essential ideas in a lesson or unit. They focus student attention on the topic at hand and help them draw connections between what they already know and the new knowledge to be learned.

Schoen and Schoen (2003) recommend advance organizers, noting that they help ELL students understand key concepts that they will be exposed to in a text. For example, when webs are used as advance organizers, students can see connections between words or phrases and the topic by following symbols and arrows.

Generalizations from *Classroom Instruction That Works*

Four generalizations are identified in the research on advance organizers:

1. As is the case with cues and questions, advance organizers should focus on what is important instead of what is unusual.
2. Again as with cues and questions, higher-level advance organizers produce deeper learning than lower-level advance organizers.
3. Advance organizers are best used to give structure to information that is not well organized.
4. There are four main types of advance organizers: expository, narrative, skimming, and graphic. Different types of organizers can be used for different purposes and produce different results.

Because advance organizers help students organize new information, they are particularly helpful for students at early stages of language acquisition. Students should be introduced to each of the four main types of advance organizers, as each of them produces different results.

Classroom Recommendations

There are four recommendations for using these four types of advance organizers in the classroom.

1. Use expository advance organizers because they describe the new content that will be introduced. Expository advance organizers are a clear-cut, uncomplicated means of describing the new content students will be learning.

Before having ELLs in his class, 5th grade science teacher Mr. Abrams used an expository advance organizer to teach an activity as follows:

> Mr. Abrams tells students in his science class that he is going to float a potato in the center of a beaker of clear liquid. He wants them to apply what they already know about density and solubility to figure out why the potato floats.
>
> Mr. Abrams explains that he will place three beakers on a table in front of the room and fill each with a slightly different solution. All the solutions will appear clear, says Mr. Abrams, but one beaker will be filled with plain water, another will contain a very strong sugar and water solution, and the third will be filled half with the sugar/water solution and half with water.
>
> Next, says Mr. Abrams, he will cut a potato into one-inch wedges and place one wedge in each beaker. In one beaker, the wedge will float on the top, in one it will sink to the bottom, and in one it will float right in the center of the liquid. Mr. Abrams challenges his students to figure out which solution is which and why the trick works.

Here is how Mr. Abrams modified the activity for use with ELLs:

> Mr. Abrams knows that he cannot just tell his science students what they are going to do. He needs to explain it to them using sheltering techniques, including
>
> • Manipulatives, miniature objects, and realia
> • Visuals (photos, pictures, drawings)
> • Body movement and pantomime

- Facial expressions and gestures
- Clear expression and articulation
- Shorter, simpler sentences
- Eye contact
- High-frequency vocabulary
- Reduction of idiomatic expressions
- Personalized language and nouns favored over pronouns
- Synonyms

Mr. Abrams tells his students that he is going to "float" a potato in the center of a beaker of clear liquid. He wants them to apply what they already know about density and solubility to figure out why the potato floats.

In addition to orally explaining that he is going to fill each of the three beakers with a different solution, he pantomimes the act. When describing the different solutions, Mr. Abrams shows a drawing of plain water, another of water and sugar, and a third of a beaker filled half with the sugar/water solution and half with water.

As he tells his students about the potato, Mr. Abrams actually cuts a potato into one-inch wedges and pantomimes placing a potato wedge in each beaker. He continues to use body movements to let everyone know that in one beaker the potato will float on the top, in one it will sink to the bottom, and in one it will float right in the center of the liquid. Mr. Abrams challenges his students to figure out which solution is which and why the trick works.

2. Use narrative advance organizers to let students know what they are going to be learning in a story format. Because Mr. Anderson was going to be starting a 3rd grade unit on the experiences of immigrant groups as they moved to the United States, he told students the following story:

My grandfather Gustav came here from Sweden with his cousin, Nels, in the late 1800s. They were young kids, 18 or 19 years old. They had been farmers in Sweden, but there was a potato famine and thousands of Swedes immigrated to the United States about that same time. I've often thought what a spirit of adventure they must have had.

Somehow Grandpa Gus and cousin Nels made it to Minneapolis, where Grandpa Gus met a girl named Brynhild, whom he married. Grandma Bryn also was from Sweden. When I was little, we would go to their house to celebrate

Santa Lucia Day, near Christmas. One of my cousins would get to wear a beautiful white dress and a garland of lighted candles on her head. There was always a huge table full of food. There was one kind of fish that was very stinky, but there were also lots of delicious cookies and cakes. Like other immigrants, we were celebrating our heritage but also making new traditions in the United States.

In a classroom with English-only students, a teacher could essentially stand in front of the room and tell this story. With ELLs, however, and particularly with Preproduction students, this would simply sound like noise. Remember when a teacher would talk to Charlie Brown and all he would hear was "Wa-wa, wa-wa-wa-wa?" That's how English can sound to these students. By using sheltering techniques such as visuals, pantomime, and simple vocabulary, teachers can bring understanding and comprehensibility to the story.

3. Use skimming before reading as a form of advance organizer.
The Survey, Question, Read, Recite, and Review (or SQ3R) strategy (Robinson, 1961) has long been popular with ESL teachers because it engages students in each phase of the reading process, including skimming. This activity will need to be teacher-directed and modeled before students can do it on their own. Provide students with the following directions for the activity.

Step 1: Survey what you are about to read.
- Think about the title: What do you know about this subject? What do you want to know?
- Glance over headings or skim the first sentences of paragraphs.
- Look at illustrations and graphic aids.
- Read the first paragraph.
- Read the last paragraph or summary.

Step 2: Question.
- Turn the title into a question. Answering this question becomes the major purpose for your reading.
- Write down any questions that come to mind during the survey.
- Turn headings into questions.
- Turn subheadings, illustrations, and graphic aids into questions.
- Write down unfamiliar vocabulary and determine the meaning.

Step 3: Read actively.
- Read to search for answers to questions.

The kids call it "skim and scan." They use it as kind of an initial glance over, looking at the title and captions, and looking for bolded and italicized words, and looking at the pictures. Just kind of a quick glance to predict what it is going to be about. Then I try to tap into their background knowledge at some point with that.

—Eliza Sorte,
Berry Creek Middle School,
Edwards, Colorado

The science textbook has great pictures and little figures and captions that go with each section, so we cover a whole section and just look at the pictures and talk about those for a little bit. We spend some time talking about what do you see here, how might that go along with the earth's changing surface, and what we are going to talk about, weather erosion. Then we start to think that way—think ahead and plan what might come up, and anticipate what we might see in the text and learn about.

—Adam Schmucker,
Berry Creek Middle School,
Edwards, Colorado

- Respond to questions and use the context clues for unfamiliar words.
- React to unclear passages, confusing terms, and questionable statements by generating additional questions.

Step 4: Recite.
- Look away from the answers and the book to recall what was read.
- Recite answers to questions aloud or in writing.
- Reread text for unanswered questions.

Step 5: Review.
- Answer the major purpose questions.
- Look over answers and all parts of the chapter to organize information.
- Summarize the information learned by creating a graphic organizer that depicts the main ideas, drawing a flowchart, writing a summary, participating in a group discussion, or writing an explanation of how the material has changed your perceptions or applies to your life.

Preproduction
Students will be learning to preview text material by looking at bold print, pictures, and graphics.

Early Production
Students will be learning academic vocabulary such as headings, paragraphs, and questions.

Speech Emergence
Students will be learning how to formulate questions as they hear students turn headings, subheadings, illustrations, and graphic aids into questions.

Intermediate and Advanced Fluency
Students will be able to apply the strategy to text after the teacher has modeled, and students understand, each step.

4. Teach students how to use graphic advance organizers. Graphic advance organizers are visual representations of the information students are about to learn. These visual representations help students understand the confusing relationships presented in the text.

Classroom Example

Subject: Science
Content Objective: To classify organisms.

Mr. Henry's 6th grade class was about to view a video on arthropods. Before showing the video, Mr. Henry gave each student a graphic advance organizer with the main ideas filled in, cueing students about the information they'd be seeing (see Figure 5.2). He asked students to listen and watch carefully so they could add to the organizers as they watched the video. Specifically, he wanted students to add important information related to the ideas on the organizer, as well as other main ideas or topics.

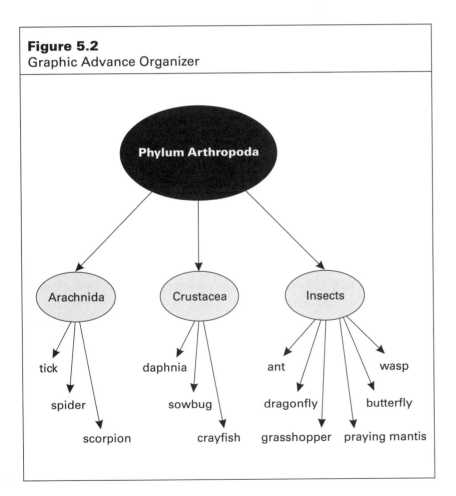

Figure 5.2
Graphic Advance Organizer

Preproduction
Students need to learn vocabulary; for these students, pictures should be attached to the labels. During the class discussion, when others are adding important information, you can engage these students

I think that with second-language learners, a graphic organizer helps because not only does the organizer give them a framework for the information, but I also think it's easier for them to make those connections. Semantic webs are good because sometimes ELLs don't have the vocabulary, but the teacher's organization of the information can help them attach meaning to it.

—*E. B.*

nonverbally by having them point to various vocabulary pictorial representations.

Early Production
Students should be using vocabulary, so they can be prompted with directives such as "Name a kind of insect."

Speech Emergence
Students will be able to demonstrate good comprehension of the video, especially since they have the advance organizer with pictures. Their contributions to the class discussion will be formatted in phrases and short sentences. They can be prompted by being asked to explain what they have seen.

Intermediate and Advanced Fluency
Students will be able to add important information related to the ideas on the organizer.

Summary

By using cues and questions, you can affect what students will learn by helping them make connections between what they already know and what they will need to know. Advance organizers also help students use their personal experiences and content knowledge to learn new information by organizing it into a visual format. Both of these means of helping ELLs access and activate background knowledge will aid them in the continuous process of acquiring and integrating content in a new language.

6

COOPERATIVE LEARNING

Mainstream teachers with both ELLs and English-dominant students in their classrooms can use cooperative learning strategies as a powerful tool for fostering language acquisition. According to most writers, there are a number of elements that set cooperative learning apart from other grouping techniques (Cochran, 1989; Johnson & Johnson, 1999). These elements include the following:

- Heterogeneous grouping (combining ELLs and English-dominant students in the same group)
- Positive interdependence (sinking or swimming together)
- Face-to-face supportive interaction (helping each other learn and applauding each other's successes and efforts)
- Individual accountability (requiring each group member to contribute to the group's achievement of its goals; typically, each member is assigned a specific role to perform in the group)
- Interpersonal and small group skills (communication, trust, leadership, decision making, and conflict resolution)
- Group processing (reflecting on how well the team is functioning and how it can function even better)

Educators have found that cooperative learning groups foster language acquisition in ways that whole-class instruction cannot. So what is it about these groups that make them such a rich opportunity for ELLs?

First, ELLs working in small groups have many more opportunities to speak than they have during whole-class instruction. Small groups "create opportunities for sustained dialogue and substantive language use" as students use language to accomplish the task at hand (Zehler, 1994, p. 7). In fact, cooperative learning groups "demand speech" because each member must carry out her role if the group as a whole is to succeed (Alanis, 2004, p. 222). Some roles you can assign and will need to thoroughly explain include recorder, final copy scribe, illustrator, materials collector, and reporter.

Group members must also "negotiate meaning" as they speak, meaning that they must adjust their language so that it is comprehensible to other members. In doing this, students ensure that all members are able to understand what others have said (Englander, 2002; Kagan, 1995). Because students are in small groups, it is easy to check for understanding and adjust the level of speech appropriately—something that a teacher or student cannot do easily in a whole-class session (Kagan, 1995).

Small groups offer the following additional advantages:

- **They allow for the repetition of key words and phrases.** According to Kagan (1995), "Language acquisition is not ensured unless input is received repeatedly from a variety of sources." Repetition allows the ELL to move the content she hears "from short-term comprehension to long-term acquisition" (Kagan, 1995).
- **They require functional, context-relevant speech.** Speech that is personally relevant and related to "real-life" situations is more likely to add to an ELL's fluency (Kagan, 1995).
- **They are "feedback-rich."** Not only are there far more opportunities for feedback and correction in a small group setting, but the feedback and correction occur in the context of actual conversation, rather than in a formal instructional situation. An English language learner is less likely to feel self-conscious about being corrected in a small group setting (Kagan, 1995).
- **They can greatly reduce student anxiety.** Because small groups are supportive and interdependent, ELLs feel more comfortable speaking. As noted in Chapter 9, negative emotions (such as anxiety and lack of self-confidence) can impede language acquisition.

Bear in mind, however, that students who have recently arrived in the United States may be unfamiliar with group work. Kagan and McGroarty (1993) emphasize the importance of team-building exercises in creating a supportive classroom environment for these new students.

Generalizations from *Classroom Instruction That Works*

Three generalizations can be drawn about cooperative learning from *Classroom Instruction That Works*.

1. Cooperative learning groups should rarely be organized by ability. Groups should be heterogeneous—they should include both ELLs and English-dominant students. The ELLs will benefit greatly from being grouped with English-dominant students who can model correct English. Students in mixed groups also need to negotiate meaning. As ELLs strive to convey information, English-dominant students can scaffold language development by helping them find the right word or verb tense. They can also ask ELLs questions to elicit further speech.

2. Cooperative learning groups should be small. This makes sense for all students, but particularly for ELLs, who will feel more comfortable speaking in their new language in the confines of a small group of peers.

3. Although cooperative learning groups should be used regularly, teachers should take care not to overuse them. It is important to keep in mind that English language learners need time to independently practice the skills and processes that they must master.

Classroom Recommendations

There are four classroom recommendations regarding cooperative learning reviewed in *Classroom Instruction That Works*.

1. Teachers should use a variety of criteria for grouping students. Heterogeneous student teams maximize intercultural communication and increase possibilities for peer tutoring. There may also be times, however, when ELLs will profit from being grouped according to

Cooperative learning is perfect for students who are acquiring English. For example, I put one of my ELLs in a mixed group with students much higher than her and much lower than her. She is being challenged by having to explain what she is thinking to the lower ones, but she is also gaining knowledge by the language that the higher students are using. The ELLs find ways to say what they are thinking; they pick up vocabulary, and they learn how to say something from what the other students say. I think that grouping is definitely an essential component for students who are still learning English.

—L. M.

language needs depending on goals and instructional objectives. If you have students with a similar primary language, a homogeneous grouping may be beneficial, particularly at the early stages of language acquisition. Since cognitive processes are taking place in their heads (and not in English), a group of like-language users can work to clarify content and stimulate discussion at a deeper level.

2. There are several types of cooperative learning groups that will help you vary group makeup. There are informal groups; formal groups, which last long enough for students to complete an academic assignment; and base groups, which are long-term and provide members with support throughout a semester or school year.

3. Teachers should manage group size. As discussed above, small groups are generally better than larger groups. This is particularly true for ELLs because the small groups increase talk time.

4. Combine cooperative learning groups with other types of classroom instruction. Cooperative learning groups should be used intermittently along with other types of lessons, as students also need time to practice skills on their own.

Classroom Example

Take a look at the example below to see how you can implement cooperative learning in your classroom with ELLs at varying stages of language acquisition.

Subject: Science
Content Objective: To know how natural causes change the world.
      Mr. Higuera's 3rd grade class was engaged in a science unit studying how natural causes change the land and how these land changes then affect the world. After learning about the composition of rocks and how they change and about different landforms (e.g., mountains, canyons, plains, plateaus, islands), students were assigned to groups of four for a "jigsaw" activity.
      Each student on a home team selected one natural cause for which to be responsible: water (e.g., rain, rivers), ice (e.g., hail, glaciers), wind (e.g., tornadoes, hurricanes), or force (e.g., volcanoes, earthquakes). Students then were reorganized into three-person, topic-alike teams (i.e., water, ice, wind, and force teams) to begin learning about the natural causes of change, how these changes subsequently change the land, examples of the changes, and how the land changes eventually change the world.

After the initial learning—which included students visiting different centers in the classroom that contained resources and information, reading information from two texts, watching a video, and checking a Web site on the Internet—students returned to their home teams, where they shared what they had learned about their particular natural cause and the changes it made. Each student was responsible for orally presenting and teaching the information to the home group, as well as providing an artifact of his findings (e.g., an essay and a physical or pictorial representation).

Once all of the students had presented their individual information, Mr. Higuera asked the home teams to do an assignment entitled "Natural causes change the land; these changes change the world." He introduced the assignment as follows:

> In your home team, prepare a group presentation in which you provide specific examples of this statement. Each team member must participate in the presentation in some way—that is, do part of the oral presentation, create a physical or pictorial representation to be used in the presentation, or write something to go along with the presentation. Be sure to include examples of all the different natural causes and the landforms you learned about, and tell us how the changes in land have changed or are changing the world.

The above activity could be modified for each stage of language acquisition.

Preproduction

Students can join the English-dominant students in developing physical or pictorial representations to share with their home groups and use in the group presentation. When sharing, these students can point to important parts of their representations, as they may not have all the vocabulary needed to explain the natural cause and its consequences. Preproduction students should not be expected to produce an essay, although they can copy words down to use as labels for their representations.

Early Production

Students will be able to connect with the English-dominant students when devising physical or pictorial representations to share with the home team. Plan for all students to go beyond the physical and pictorial by including graphic and kinesthetic representations as well as mental images. Early Production students can use nonlinguistic representations in the group presentation, along with single words and two-word phrases. Their essays should consist of sentence starters that they complete with one or two words.

Speech Emergence

Students can read information from texts, particularly when they include graphs and pictures to aid in comprehension. These students will be less reliant on nonlinguistic representations for sharing with their home groups or in the presentations and can use sentences in explaining their examples. Their essays will reflect the sentences used in their explanations.

Intermediate and Advanced Fluency

Students can participate in all activities and work alongside English-dominant students to develop nonlinguistic representations. They will also be able to compose essays to go along with their artifacts. Expect to hear and see some errors as Intermediate Fluency students speak and write; fewer errors will occur with those students in the Advanced Fluency stage.

Now that you know what ELLs can do with the academic content, you can help further develop their language skills by remembering to implement the Word-MES formula. These students use a host of cognitive processes for learning vocabulary, including associative skills, memory, and inferential skills, to figure out what words mean based on what they look or sound like.

Preproduction

Students need help with word selection (e.g., *rain, rivers, hail, glaciers, tornadoes, hurricanes*).

Early Production

Students will benefit from you modeling correct English. Listen for any errors and remember to avoid overt corrections. If you hear students say "ail" for "hail," for example, you can model the correct pronunciation by saying, "That is a picture of hail."

Speech Emergence

Students need to have their language development stimulated, which you can accomplish by helping them put together more complex sentences. When they are developing their essays, for example, you can help them expand their English by looking for sentences that can be combined with conjunctions.

Intermediate and Advanced Fluency
Students need to work on sounding like a book. Listen to their oral presentations and help them by using synonyms for words that they already know. Also, make sure that they are not starting every sentence the same way, either in the oral presentation or in the essay.

When in doubt about what to do with ELLs at different levels, select any one of the Word-MES strategies. Any student will benefit from vocabulary growth, modeling of correct English, expanding English sentences to include more complex structures, and developing academic language that makes one sound like a book.

Summary

The jigsaw activity classroom example is a good illustration of a strategy that includes the key elements of cooperative learning. This activity adeptly shows how cooperative learning can help foster language acquisition for ELLs.

7

SUMMARIZING AND NOTE TAKING

Though there has historically been a great deal of emphasis on learning strategies, too few ELLs receive instruction in the use of thinking skills essential to summarizing and note taking (Padrón, 1992). Many teachers mistakenly believe that these higher-level skills cannot be taught to students until they have full mastery of English (Garcia & Pearson, 1991). In fact, a 1992 study by Padrón found that ELLs can benefit from learning cognitive strategies.

Summarizing

Summarizing as a learning strategy permeates Chamot and O'Malley's (1994) Cognitive Academic Language Learning Approach, which includes explicit instructions for mainstreamed ELL students. According to Short (1994), when ELLs are taught to understand text patterns (e.g., chronological and cause-and-effect patterns in history books) and recognize the signal words accompanying them, reading and writing skills improve.

Generalizations from
Classroom Instruction That Works

Three generalizations can be gleaned from the research on summarizing in *Classroom Instruction That Works*.

1. To effectively summarize, students must keep, delete, and substitute information. To enable this process, students should be taught steps or an explicit set of rules that help them develop a summary. While teaching this process, you will need to accompany the steps with nonlinguistic representations, so that each step will hold meaning for Preproduction and Early Production students. Other students will benefit from the nonlinguistic representations as well.

2. To effectively keep, delete, and substitute information, students must analyze the information at a fairly deep level. You will have already adapted the keep-delete-substitute strategy for Preproduction and Early Production students when you substitute common, frequently used vocabulary terms for unknown vocabulary terms. To help Speech Emergence and Intermediate and Advanced Fluency students analyze information at a deeper level, point out what is important and what is not.

3. Being aware of the explicit structure of information is an aid when summarizing. Text is usually presented according to certain structures or patterns. Being able to understand and then locate these structures and patterns will greatly aid the summarization process.

Teaching text structure requires a fairly sophisticated lesson. You will need to expose Preproduction and Early Production students to explicit structures. In order to make text structures more understandable, you can offer visual examples of text patterns (graphic organizers) and use eye contact, body movements, pantomime, facial expressions, gestures, clear expression, and clear articulation when explaining. Speech Emergence and Intermediate and Advanced Fluency students will be able to use the text patterns to summarize.

Classroom Recommendations

Classroom Instruction That Works offers three recommendations for incorporating summarization into the classroom.

1. Teach students the rule-based summarizing strategy. A particular set of steps is followed to produce a summary (e.g., keeping, deleting, and substituting information). Students will need to see this strategy modeled again and again. Attaching a nonlinguistic representation to

Summarizing does not mean showing off your memory and telling the whole story—some students can do that almost verbatim. A summary is only picking out the most important parts. So when the student tells the whole story, I say, "Let's go back and pick out the most important parts."

One of the things that I have found that is really successful for narratives is doing it comic-book style: "Here are six boxes. You need to pick out the six things in the story, and you can write in part of the box and draw a picture in part of the box." It can be all pictures for ELLs in the early stages. Most of the kids will write some and draw a picture so it looks like a little story. But since they have these six boxes, they need to pick out the six most important things; they need to be organized and in order, like you are reading a comic. That seems to work well.

—E. B.

A lot of our ELLs' parents don't speak much English, so I use this as an example of summarizing: "Let's pretend that I only speak a little bit of English. So, you have to tell me in only three sentences—and you have to keep it short so I can understand it—the three most important things so that I could understand the story even if I can't read it." I think that helps them; if they can relate it to something that is going on in their lives, then they are more able to make it more concise.

—*L. M.*

the rules will benefit early-stage ELLs (see the classroom example in Chapter 2).

2. Use summary frames. There are six types of summary frames (see Appendix B): narrative, topic-restriction-illustration, argumentation, problem/solution, conversation, and definition (see below). All summary frames have a set of questions that extract important elements from the text. The answers to the questions are then used to summarize the text.

Each style of summary frame captures the basic structure of a different type of text. For example, let's take a look at a definition frame. The purpose of a definition frame is to define a particular concept and identify other related concepts. There are four elements of a definition frame:

1. **Term:** the subject being defined
2. **Set:** the general category to which the term belongs
3. **Gross characteristics:** the characteristics that separate the term from other elements in the set
4. **Minute differences:** the different classes of objects that fall directly beneath the term

There are also four guiding questions for use when completing a definition frame:

1. What is being defined?
2. To which general category does the item belong?
3. What characteristics separate the item from the other items in the general category?
4. What are some types of classes of the item being defined?

Now let's look at an example of how a definition frame can be used with ELLs at different stages of language acquisition. Students in Mr. Tate's 3rd grade life science class are studying grasshoppers. Today, he is showing them a film. To guide their viewing, Mr. Tate presents the students with the four guiding definition frame questions listed above. For ELLs, he includes the chart depicted in Figure 7.1, with the frame questions accompanied by visuals.

Mr. Tate explains that answers to the frame questions can be found in the film. Students then watch the film with an eye toward answering the questions. When the film is over, Mr. Tate organizes the students into groups, where they compare their answers and construct a summary statement about grasshoppers.

3. Instruct students in reciprocal teaching as an aid to understanding expository text. Reciprocal teaching is a type of dialogue that

Figure 7.1
Definition Frame Chart

The definition frame tells:

1. What

2. General Category

3. Characteristics

4. Differences

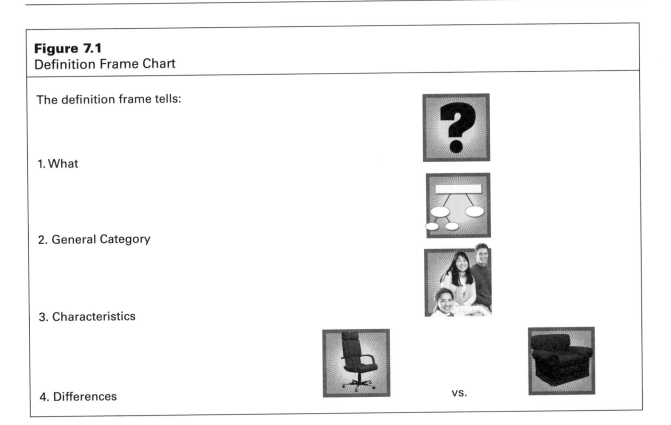

vs.

students use to create meaning from text (Palincsar & Brown, 1984). When reviewing effective instructional programs for ELLs in elementary and middle schools, Fashola, Slavin, Calderón, and Durán (1997) reported that reciprocal teaching contributed to an improvement in reading comprehension. *In the Classroom: A Toolkit for Effective Instruction of English Learners*—available through the National Clearinghouse for English Language Acquisition (n.d.b)—offers sample lessons and activities for reciprocal teaching and emphasizes the importance of modeling each step with ELLs.

Reciprocal teaching involves four components: summarizing, questioning, clarifying, and predicting. For ELLs, it is critical to model each step and check for student understanding. Once the four components are learned, students can use them to monitor their reading for better comprehension.

The following is an adaptation involving the four components of reciprocal teaching that can be used as a whole-class activity or in small groups.

- **Step 1: Summarizing.** After students have silently or orally read a short section of a passage, a single student acting as teacher (i.e., the student leader) summarizes what has been

> I made bookmarks for everyone to encourage them to use summary frames.
> —*Sandra Dreschler,*
> *Berry Creek Middle School,*
> *Edwards, Colorado*

read. Other students, with guidance from the student leader, may add to the summary. If students have difficulty summarizing, the teacher might point out clues (important items or obvious topic sentences) that aid in the construction of good summaries.

- **Step 2: Questioning.** The student leader asks some questions to which the class responds. The questions are designed to help students identify important information in the passage. For example, the student leader might look back over the selection and ask questions about specific pieces of information. The other students then try to answer these questions based on their recollection of the information.

- **Step 3: Clarifying.** The student leader tries to clarify confusing points in the passage. He might point these out or ask other students to point them out. For example, the student leader might say, "The part about why the dog ran into the car was confusing to me. Can anyone explain this?" Or the student leader might direct students to ask clarification questions. The group then attempts to clear up the confusing parts, which might involve rereading parts of the passage.

- **Step 4: Predicting.** The student leader asks for predictions about what will happen in the next segment of the text. The leader can write the predictions on the blackboard or on an overhead, or students can write them down.

Adapting the Keep-Delete-Substitute Strategy to the Stages of Language Acquisition

You can model the keep-delete-substitute strategy for summarizing by emphasizing the following steps:

1. Keep important information
2. Delete trivial material that is unnecessary to understanding
3. Delete redundant material
4. Substitute subordinate terms for more specific terms (e.g., use *fish* for *rainbow trout, salmon,* and *halibut*)
5. Select a topic sentence or invent one if it is missing

Preproduction

Students will benefit from the use of gestures every time you say "keep," "delete," or "substitute." "Keep" can be represented nonlinguistically with a quick gesture by crossing both arms over your chest. "Delete" can be shown by having one hand grab something from the other and then throw it away. For "substitute," you can place both fists in front of your chest and then move the right fist up and over the left.

I've really loved the reciprocal teaching. We made a simile for each of the different roles, so students had a pictorial representation to cue them for what those roles were. A clarifier looks at things like a magnifying glass, a summarizer wraps things up like a ball of yarn, a predictor sees into the future like a fortune-teller, and a questioner is like a detective. So I would hold up a ball of string, and they would kind of know, "Oh, I'm going to wrap things up, I'm going to summarize it."

I really liked [using reciprocal teaching] with all my kids, and my ELL kids in particular have absolutely thrived with that. They have taken to asking higher-level questions, and they are really digging deep into the text. We've talked about how you can be a reciprocal member and even work on your own, so that some of the students go through the different roles when they read things by themselves now as a method to understand and summarize the text for themselves.

—*E. S.*

Early Production

Students will need to have the substitute rule reinforced with demonstrations of how to substitute common-frequency vocabulary words (vocabulary they may already know) for low-frequency vocabulary words (vocabulary that may be new). For example, you can let these students know that Mercury, Venus, and Mars can be replaced with the word "planets."

Speech Emergence

Students have good comprehension and can follow your modeling of the keep-delete-substitute rule for summarizing, particularly with gestures, a slower rate of speech, clear and concise sentences, and demonstrations.

Intermediate and Advanced Fluency

Students will have excellent comprehension of this rule, particularly when provided with all of the above suggestions.

Adapting Summary Frames to the Stages of Language Acquisition

Mrs. Mason used the narrative frame to help her 1st graders summarize *Jack and the Beanstalk*. First, she introduced some of the following frame questions and told the students to think about them as she read the story aloud:

1. Who are the main characters? What are their characteristics?
2. When and where did the story take place? What were the circumstances?
3. What prompted the action in the story?
4. How do the main characters react emotionally to what happens at the start of the story?
5. What did the main characters decide to do? Did they set a goal? What was it?
6. How did the main characters try to accomplish their goals?
7. How does the story turn out? Did the main characters accomplish their goals?

Next, Mrs. Mason read the story again. This time, however, she occasionally stopped to let students answer the questions as a class. Finally, Mrs. Mason and the students used their answers to write a summary together.

For students with little or no English proficiency, you must create circumstances and conditions that support engagement in interpretive discussions of stories. This can be achieved through the use of tiered questions.

For reciprocal teaching, I have students prepare for all jobs initially, so they don't know what their job is going to be. Then, once they find out what their job is, they get to meet with all the summarizers, they get to meet with all the clarifiers, etc., so that if they didn't get a word or they weren't clear on something, they have another chance before they have to go back and perform that role as individuals. That's a good strategy to make it safer for ELLs so they get to do it by themselves and think by themselves first and then get paired up with a similar activity group. Then they get to perform their role individually with the rest of their team.

—D. H.

Preproduction

Students can be asked questions that start with "Show me . . .," "Point to the . . .," "Where is . . .," and "Who has the . . ." (e.g., "Show me Jack," "Point to mother," "Where is the beanstalk?" "Who has the harp?"). Remember to begin asking these students questions from the Early Production stage in order to scaffold language development.

Early Production

Students can answer yes/no questions, either/or questions, and questions requiring a one- or two-word response. Appropriate queries include who, what, when, and where questions (e.g., "Who is in this story?" "What is Jack doing now?" "When did Jack find the beanstalk—in the morning or evening?" "Where is Jack going?"). In addition to these questions, be sure to include some from the next stage.

Speech Emergence

Students can answer with short sentences. Ask them why and how questions or prompt them with "Explain . . ." and "Tell me about . . ." (e.g., "Why is Jack's mother upset?" "How do you think Jack and his mother felt?" "Explain how Jack got the gold coins," "Tell me about what Jack decided to do"). Move into the next stage of questions as well.

Intermediate and Advanced Fluency

Students can be asked any of the questions in the narrative frame. Intermediates will have a few grammatical errors in their answers, and Advanced students will sound almost like their English-dominant peers.

Adapting Reciprocal Teaching to the Stages of Language Acquisition

There are four steps to reciprocal teaching. Initially, a teacher can focus on one individual strategy at a time without adding another strategy to the repertoire until students are fairly proficient with the previous strategy. At the end of the teacher's modeling, students should be able to perform all four steps for reciprocal teaching.

- **Step 1: Generating questions.** When teaching this step to ELLs, everyone needs to learn what types of questions match the different levels of language acquisition.
- **Step 2: Summarizing.** Keep the following tips in mind when teaching this skill to students at different levels of language acquisition.

- *Preproduction*. Students will need to have key vocabulary pointed out to them. The students who are summarizing should be expected to select three words they think everyone is familiar with and three words they think might be new. The old and new words need to be accompanied by a pictorial representation, or the student assuming the teaching role can act out the words.
- *Early Production*. Students will benefit from key vocabulary and by hearing correct English modeled. You need to inform students that their summaries need to be clear and understandable.
- *Speech Emergence and Intermediate and Advanced Fluency*. Students will better comprehend the passage they are reading by creating a clear, concise summary.
- **Step 3: Clarifying.** In addition to clarifying any new vocabulary, you will need to clarify idioms and figures of speech for ELLs.
- **Step 4: Predicting.** This skill activates background knowledge and helps students draw connections between new information and things they already know.

Note Taking

Note taking is closely related to summarizing because it requires that students take information and synthesize it using their own words. The purpose of note taking is to help students acquire and integrate knowledge; it is a way to organize and process information. Because ELLs are extracting new knowledge in a new language, they will need explicit instruction in the art of note taking.

Generalizations from
Classroom Instruction That Works

Classroom Instruction That Works suggests four generalizations on note taking.

1. Verbatim note taking is the least effective way to take notes. When students write down every single word they hear, they are not engaged in synthesizing information. Trying to record everything that is said or read occupies a student's working memory and does not leave room for analyzing the incoming information.

You probably won't have to worry about early-stage ELLs taking verbatim notes, but students at all stages should be discouraged from

I think the hardest thing about note taking—and it's kind of like summarizing—is that you have to pick out what is important. A lot of times the kids will say, "I really liked that, that's interesting." I'll say, "That's interesting, but do you think that is going to be on our test?" I really have them think, "If you were the teacher, what would you pull out as being the important things?"

You have to teach kids to review their notes and how to study. You have to model that, too—walk them through how to use their notes to study. For example, "I'm going to turn to where I have fractions in my notes, and I see here that there's the numerator and there's the denominator. My teacher says that the *d* in 'denominator' is like 'downstairs.' I bet I'm going to need to know that for my fractions test."

—*E. B.*

doing so. As an alternative to having students take written notes, you can stop and ask them to draw what they understand after you have given part of a lesson.

2. Notes should always be considered works in progress. As students acquire and integrate content knowledge, they return to their notes and revise them to reflect their deeper understanding. Teachers need to explicitly teach and reinforce this process, and should allow time to make sure notes are appended and edited. For ELLs, additions to notes can mean finding other graphics to accompany teacher-prepared notes.

3. Notes should be used as study guides for tests. If notes are clear and synthesize the information adequately, they will serve students well during test preparation. When students review and revise notes, they are studying the content. It is important to verify that ELLs' notes contain visual representations.

4. The more notes taken, the better. This does not mean taking verbatim notes, but rather notes that elaborate on the learning objectives. A strong correlation exists between the amount of notes taken and student achievement on tests. For English language learners, the more graphics, the better.

Classroom Recommendations

Teachers can direct students on how to take good notes. *Classroom Instruction That Works* offers three recommendations on teaching good note-taking skills.

1. Give students teacher-prepared notes. This is the first step in modeling good note taking. When students see teacher-prepared notes, they have a clear example of what the teacher considers important. For ELLs, teacher-prepared notes can take written form with pictorial representations. As students progress in their language acquisition, notes can be given in written form with some of the words missing.

2. Teach students a variety of note-taking formats (see Figure 7.2). There is not one set way to take notes. Different students select different note-taking formats. It will be important to model all the different forms of note taking, along with clear, concise explanations.

One of the models students will learn, the informal outline, is characterized by indentations to indicate major ideas and their related details. Another model, webbing, can be valuable for ELLs because it provides a visual representation. A third type of format, combination notes (see below), uses both the informal outline and the web technique.

3. Use combination notes. Combination notes combine linguistic and nonlinguistic formats. They are particularly helpful because they allow students to portray the information in a visual way. When students are taking notes, it is helpful if you stop periodically to let them make a graphic representation. This may take extra time, but it forces students to consider the information a second time. It also allows students to store the information in a different way without using words.

Figure 7.3 shows how a page of notes is divided into three parts. The left side is used for informal outlining, and the right side is reserved for a web or some variation of it. Finally, the bottom of the page is saved for a summary statement. Figure 7.4 depicts another type of combination notes that is especially useful for ELLs.

Adapting Teacher-Prepared Notes to the Stages of Language Acquisition

Figure 7.5 shows an example of teacher-prepared notes for mainstream students. Follow the suggestions below to use these notes with all stages of ELLs.

Preproduction
Students can participate in a whole-class discussion on teacher notes when a student completes the graphic part of the chart. You can ask these students to respond nonverbally with "Show me . . ." or "Point to . . . ." For practice, these students can use the teacher-prepared notes and select words they know and do not know. You can also provide students with ways to keep track of their new words (e.g., three-ring binder, spiral notebook, or note cards).

Early Production
Students can also participate in a whole-class discussion when someone completes the graphic part of the notes. Ask yes/no questions or questions requiring one- or two-word responses, such as "Do ants have antennae?" These students can also practice familiar and unfamiliar vocabulary words.

Speech Emergence
Students can answer why, how, when, or where questions using the teacher-prepared written notes and graphics.

I think note taking starts as teacher-generated note taking. We had our little math notebooks at the beginning of the year, and I really wrote everything on the board that I wanted in their notebooks. Then slowly but surely I asked, "Well, what do you think is important? Write it in your notebook if you think it's important to remember. We have a quiz on Friday on fractions; make sure you are getting down what you need to have so you can study."

—D. H.

I do have to model note taking for all kids. Note taking, I think, is hard—especially for 6th graders, as they haven't done a lot of it yet. We will read something together and pick out the most important things and write those on the right. For ELLs, I've usually prewritten it myself, then I give them the notes but without some of the words. Then they will see it on the overhead, and they can fill in a few missing words on each note.

I also try to draw pictures more with my ELLs with each part of our notes. I'm not a very good artist, so they get a whole lot of laughs then. But they can draw their own pictures and put them in their notes.

—Sheri Daigler,
Berry Creek Middle School,
Edwards, Colorado

Figure 7.2
Types of Note-Taking Formats

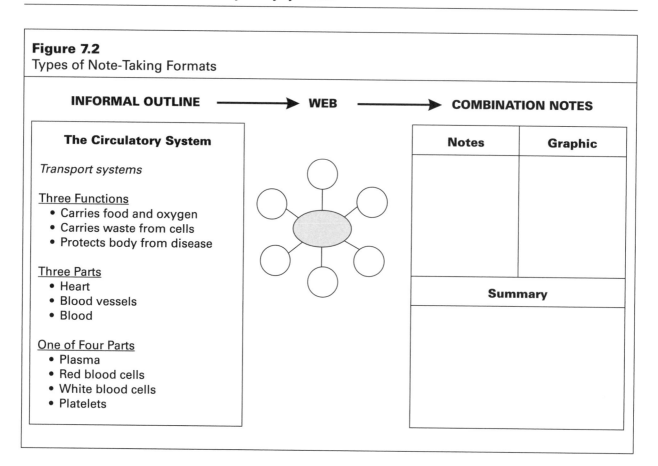

INFORMAL OUTLINE ⟶ WEB ⟶ COMBINATION NOTES

The Circulatory System

Transport systems

<u>Three Functions</u>
• Carries food and oxygen
• Carries waste from cells
• Protects body from disease

<u>Three Parts</u>
• Heart
• Blood vessels
• Blood

<u>One of Four Parts</u>
• Plasma
• Red blood cells
• White blood cells
• Platelets

Notes	Graphic

Summary

Intermediate Fluency
Students can respond to teacher questions that start with "Why do you think . . . ."

Advanced Fluency
Students can write questions (see the third column of Figure 7.5). While you are engaging early- to mid-level ELLs in answering questions, English-dominant students and Advanced Fluency students are writing questions.

Adapting Other Note-Taking Formats to the Stages of Language Acquisition

After 3rd through 6th grade students have learned a variety of note-taking formats, develop work stations for each. Students should try each type of format before coming together for a whole-group discussion on what worked best for them.

Figure 7.3
Combination Notes

Notes	Graphic Representation
Clouds	

Four types of clouds

High
   cirrus: feathery
   cirrostratus: fine, like a white veil or
     a halo
   cirrocumulus: small fleecy balls and
     wisps

Middle
   altostratus: thick gray or blue veil
   altocumulus: dense fleecy balls/puffs

Low
   stratocumulus: big rolls, soft gray

Vertical
   cumulus: shaped like a dome
   cumulonimbus: dark, heavy-looking

Summary: There are four types of clouds. They vary in shape and color.

Figure 7.4
Combination Notes for ELLs

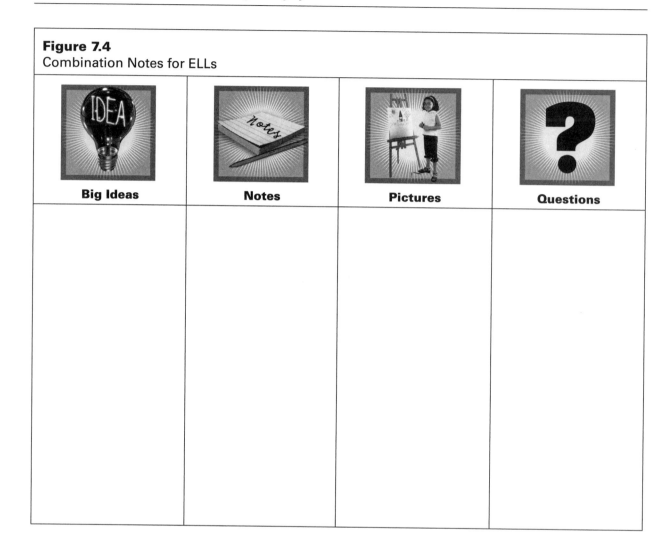

Big Ideas	Notes	Pictures	Questions

Preproduction

Students will take notes that focus on words, so a fourth work station will be beneficial for them as they engage in various vocabulary activities with the words. How do you select words to be learned? Students whose native languages are based largely on Greek or Latin should be encouraged to infer the meaning of unfamiliar English words by using their knowledge of cognates—words that sound and look the same in both languages. For instance, a student who knows the meaning of the Spanish word *insectos* can infer the meaning of the English word *insects*. Most English content-area words have a Greek or Latin base and are similar in Spanish (e.g., *adición* = addition, *gravedad* = gravity, *observar* = to observe). Of course, students whose native languages differ significantly from English will not be able to use this word identification technique.

Figure 7.5
Teacher-Prepared Notes

Notes	Graphic	Questions
I. The Basics A. Ants are part of a family of insects that have a very orga-nized social life. B. Nearly 9,000 species exist. C. Ants are found around the world, except in the polar regions and at the highest altitudes.		
II. Characteristics A. Ants are related to wasps—have abdo-men that is jointed to the thorax by a "pedicel." B. Have antennae with "elbows" or joints in the middle. C. Some ants have a stinger that is used to defend the colony or themselves. D. Many species secrete a type of acid that is a strong repellent.		

Early Production
Students will also be concentrating on words when taking notes.

Speech Emergence
Students will work on expanding their written notes by adding essen-tial adjectives or phrases to their notes. They are likely to need your help with this.

Intermediate and Advanced Fluency
Students will work in all different note-taking formats. You will need to find teachable moments to develop their academic language.

Summary

With appropriate modifications, both summarizing and note taking can be effective strategies for ELLs. Summarizing techniques work best when the teacher uses comprehensible input, such as visuals and kinesthetic clues, while keeping in mind the appropriate questioning strategies for each stage of language acquisition. Reciprocal teaching is a particularly effective form of summarizing when working with ELLs.

Note taking works well when you encourage students to supplement their written notes with visual representations. Combining linguistic and nonlinguistic learning increases the likelihood that knowledge will be stored and retained.

8

HOMEWORK AND PRACTICE

Homework

Homework provides students with opportunities to practice, review, and apply knowledge. Given that "schooling occupies only about 13 percent of the waking hours in the first 18 years of life" (Fraser, Walberg, Welch, & Hattie, 1987, p. 234), homework is an effective means of extending student learning beyond the school day.

There are some general guidelines to keep in mind regarding homework for ELLs. In its online resource, *In the Classroom: A Toolkit for Effective Instruction of English Learners* (n.d.b), the National Clearinghouse for English Language Acquisition (NCELA) recommends that mainstream K–6 teachers include the following items to help ensure that homework assignments will be understood and accomplished:

- Concrete, nonlinguistic examples such as photographs, objects, visual organizers, graphics, demonstrations, notes, or outlines
- Opportunities for students to ask questions and discuss assignments orally
- Native language support through bilingual tutors, instructions, or materials

- Peer support for note taking and homework
- Modified or additional instructions
- Tips and strategies for learning

In another online resource, *In the Classroom: Guiding Principles* (n.d.c), NCELA advises teachers to make time available for ELLs to ask questions about the homework and receive further explanations from the teacher. Students will better understand their assignments if you provide clear and concise directions, post the assignment on the board, and offer visual organizers.

Homework can be modified for ELLs by reducing complexity and increasing applicability. For example, Echevarria and Graves (1998) suggest shortening the list of science terms on a study sheet (reduced complexity) or extending the due date (increased applicability). Appropriate homework assignments require students to practice things they have already learned in the classroom, such as vocabulary, concepts, or written language activities.

Generalizations from *Classroom Instruction That Works*

Classroom Instruction That Works suggests four generalizations from the research on homework practices.

1. The amount of homework assigned to students should increase as they progress from elementary school through high school.

2. Parental involvement in homework should be minimal. Parents can support their children by providing the place, time, and resources for their children to engage in homework. They can also offer feedback and prompts as homework is being worked on. If students can do their homework independently, then it has been assigned at an appropriate level.

Special homework issues arise with parents of ELLs. For example, some parents hesitate to discuss homework with their children because they do not understand the language of the assignment. You should always encourage parents to use their native language at home. If a student tells a parent that she's studying earthquakes, for example, the parent probably will not describe plate tectonics but may relate a personal story of experiencing an earthquake. When parents use their native language to relate a story, their narrative will be rich with vocabulary and explanations.

Parents should be encouraged to model literacy in their native language as well. Because native language development may not occur during the school day, opportunities for primary language growth at home become even more important. Years of research stress the importance of a strong foundation in the primary language in helping students acquire another language.

3. The purpose of homework should be identified and articulated. There are two reasons for homework: to practice or elaborate on what has been learned and to prepare for new information. ELLs do not have to receive the same homework as English-dominant students. In fact, if they are given the exact same homework, they may be using unfamiliar skills or incorrectly practicing them. Students should be given homework that requires them to use what they already know or what they are learning.

4. Feedback should be provided on homework assignments. It is not always the teacher who has to make the comments; students can offer feedback to one another. Such peer feedback can be helpful for ELLs, provided that students are not inundated with advice from English-dominant students on how to correct every single error.

Classroom Recommendations

There are three recommendations about homework from the research.

1. Establish and communicate a homework policy. Homework policies should inform students and parents about the purpose of homework, estimate the amount of homework that students will typically receive, discuss consequences for not turning in assignments, and suggest ways in which parents can help. For ELLs, whenever possible, be sure to send this policy home in a language that their parents can understand.

2. Design homework assignments that clearly articulate the purpose and outcome. When ELLs are in mainstream classrooms, their homework assignments will vary depending on their level of language proficiency. All students should understand the purpose of each assignment. Some assignments may be for practicing or elaborating on vocabulary or other knowledge and skills already learned in school, while others will focus on preparing students for new information or will elaborate on information that has already been introduced.

3. Feedback should be varied. As noted above, students can discuss homework with each other as well as with teachers. ELLs will benefit from seeing examples of homework from other students and hearing the explanations provided.

Many students were English language learners, and they were at all different levels. So a lot of the time it would be, "You are going to do it at your level." The homework is based on what they can do and what they can choose. So if they choose a writing assignment—to write about what they did last weekend using complete sentences, for example—it might be seven sentences from one person, whereas for somebody who is [in Speech Emergence], it might be just two sentences. They still put in the same amount of effort or time. We would talk about it: "Your homework should take you no more than 30 minutes. If it takes you more than 30 minutes, then something is going on, and we need to have a discussion as a teacher and student." I think they did really well with that. They felt ownership of what they were doing.

—D. H.

Adapting Homework to the Stages of Language Acquisition

In general, stage-appropriate questioning strategies and the Word-MES formula will be your best guides to determining appropriate homework and feedback for your ELLs. Let's look at how this works when commenting on homework—an area where the Word-MES formula is particularly appropriate.

Preproduction

Students will benefit from a peer helping them with word selection (i.e., vocabulary) on their homework assignment. Homework for students at this level may be different than everyone else's because it could focus on vocabulary. This is fine, as students need to learn the vocabulary of a topic before they can make sense of the content.

Early Production

Students can make gains in English proficiency if classmates model correct grammar for them. One way to do this is to allow ELL students to examine homework completed by English-dominant students.

Speech Emergence

Students can also benefit from explanations given by English-dominant students on how to expand or combine sentences on a homework assignment.

Intermediate and Advanced Fluency

Students can share their ideas with English-dominant students, which will help to broaden their knowledge base and improve homework assignments as they use academic English and begin to "sound like a book."

Classroom Example

Subject: Social Studies

Content Objective: To recognize a variety of influences on consumers and how these influences affect decisions about purchases.

Students have already discovered that they are surrounded by images and messages telling them what to buy, what is better, what tastes better, and so forth. They have also explored the creators of these images and messages, and the audiences they are targeting. Students chose a product as a whole-class activity and then discussed and demonstrated advertisers' claims about the product (e.g., it tastes good, improves health, is fast-acting). They also talked about how the advertisers got the audience's attention and what factors induced the students to buy the product. They pointed out pictures or words that persuade consumers. They discussed and brought in examples of advertising from various media sources (e.g., TV, radio, billboards, flyers, signs at grocery stores, newspapers, magazines, the Internet, coupons).

After much discussion, demonstration, and classroom activities, the following homework was assigned. Students were asked to gather examples of advertising that influenced a purchase made by their mother or father or one that incited the students themselves to convince their parents to buy a product for them. The students then were asked to either draw or write a description of that experience. They were also given the choice of writing about an ad they saw on TV, heard on the radio, or saw in a magazine that was convincing, and discussing how it was convincing (e.g., message, presentation, price). The teacher was careful to set a reasonable expectation for this assignment by stating how many paragraphs were expected and by emphasizing that drawings should illustrate what was convincing about the advertisement.

Preproduction

Students can practice words for items they studied during class by finding or drawing another example from home. For example, when the class talks about Nike shoes, students learn the words "toe," "heel," "shoelaces," and "swoosh." For homework, they can draw a shoe and label the parts (see Figure 8.1). They can also be assigned to

Figure 8.1
Homework Adapted for Preproduction Students

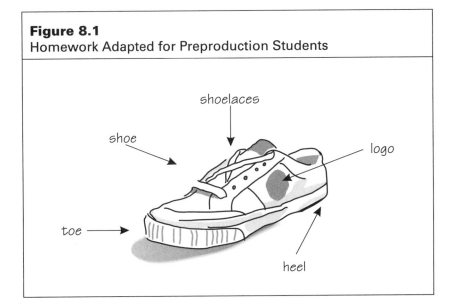

draw and label five items from home that have been discussed in class. Any word selection activity you can provide will keep them in the learning loop. You can then assess vocabulary with statements such as "Show me the toe" or "Point to the shoelaces."

Early Production
Students can also use practice with vocabulary. In addition to nouns, they should be working on vocabulary for sight, touch, sound, taste, and smell. For homework, they can select four items from home and practice writing their new vocabulary in the chart provided (see Figure 8.2).

Figure 8.2
Homework Adapted for Early Production Students

Product Name:		Item #1	Item #2	Item #3	Item #4
Sight	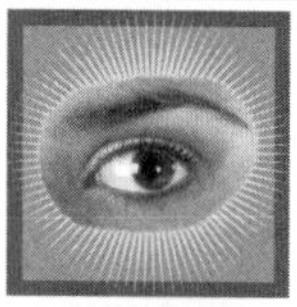				
Sound	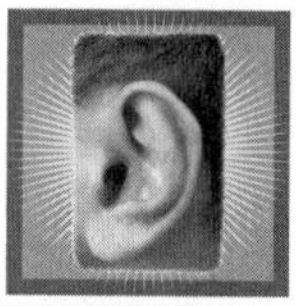				
Taste					
Smell	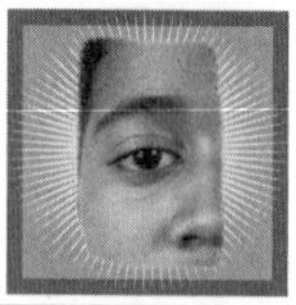				
Feel					

Speech Emergence
Students can select items from home and complete the chart depicted in Figure 8.3. The first row gives an example for students.

Intermediate and Advanced Fluency
Students can draw something they saw on TV and describe why it was convincing according to at least three criteria (e.g., message, presentation, and price).

Figure 8.3
Homework Adapted for Speech Emergence Students

Product Name	Why did you buy it?	Why do you think you like it?
EXAMPLE: *Cap'n Crunch cereal*	EXAMPLE: I bought it because *I saw it on TV.*	EXAMPLE: I like it because *it has sugar. The box is cool.*

Practice

Students practice to deepen their understanding of content and to become proficient at skills. During practice, teachers can carefully point out errors and common difficulties so students do not continue to make mistakes.

Students should practice skills or processes so that they can attain automaticity. It is up to you, as the teacher, to decide what is worth practicing. You must then also make sure enough time is available to engage in practice.

When it comes to ELLs, practice is particularly important. You do not want students spending too much energy on certain skills and not enough on others when time is of the essence (as with older ELLs). Choosing practice activities carefully helps make the time you have with these students more productive and focused.

Generalizations from *Classroom Instruction That Works*

Although we found no literature that focused specifically on the role of practice for ELLs, the authors of *Classroom Instruction That Works* examined two generalizations in this area. These generalizations are as applicable to ELLs as they are to English-dominant students.

1. Mastering a skill or a process entails focused practice. If English-dominant students need to practice a skill or process at least 24 times to obtain 80 percent proficiency (Anderson, 1995; Newell & Rosenbloom, 1981), then ELLs need even more focused practice, some of which can be assigned for homework.

2. During practice, students should adapt and shape what they have learned. Multiple practice sessions allow students to familiarize themselves with the steps involved in learning a skill or process. During this learning time, ELLs should not be pressed for speed; instead, you should attend to these students by slowly walking them through a few practice examples and providing immediate feedback.

Classroom Recommendations

Classroom Instruction That Works suggests three approaches to classroom practice with this strategy.

1. Ask students to chart their speed and accuracy. Some skills depend on speed, and some depend on accuracy. Telling time is a skill requiring both speed *and* accuracy; converting metrics to standard English measurement requires accuracy but not speed. This recommendation would not apply to early- to mid-stage ELLs, but it can be introduced to Intermediate Fluency students and used with Advanced Fluency students.

2. Design practice that focuses on specific elements of a complex skill or process. For example, if there is a particularly difficult skill in the reading or writing process for ELLs, give them assignments that work on strengthening that one aspect.

3. Plan time for students to increase their conceptual understanding of skills or processes. There is no way to become truly fluent at a task if automaticity is not accompanied by background understanding. The reasoning behind the skill or process will need to be made explicit for ELLs; this can be accomplished through think-alouds, which let teachers use the language of reasoning as they perform and describe the steps required for a particular skill. Think-alouds contribute to conceptual understanding for ELLs.

Classroom Example

Subject: Math
Content Objective: To add and substract using pictures or stories.

Ms. Chasse's 1st grade students were excited about learning their addition and subtraction math facts, but she didn't want them to simply memorize the numbers. Ms. Chasse knew that a strong conceptual understanding of the processes of addition and subtraction would help her students as they progressed to more difficult math problems. Each time they went over a new "fact family," she reviewed what "adding" meant and what "subtracting" meant. Students worked with manipulatives and drew pictures to represent what was happening with the numbers as they performed the processes.

Students practiced their math facts for homework that night. The next day in class as they reviewed, Ms. Chasse called on students to tell a story that explained the fact.

Preproduction
Students can draw or find pictures to represent their math facts. Instead of telling a story that explains their math facts to the class, you can ask for them to respond nonverbally: "Show me one strawberry plus one strawberry equals two strawberries." This will help their word selection and vocabulary development because they are associating the spoken word with an image or a number word with their own drawing.

Early Production
Students can also share a pictorial representation of a story about their math facts. To help with their explanations, you can prompt them with yes/no questions or questions that require a one- or two-word response. Because their responses to your prompts will be limited, model English for them by telling them what you see in the picture using present tense verbs as you point to the pictures: "I see two strawberries. You eat one. Now there is only one left."

Speech Emergence

Students can tell a short story with simple sentences about their math facts. To help expand their English, you can prompt by asking "why" and "how" questions. Expand whatever they are telling in their stories with an additional adjective or phrase. If the student says, "Here is a man buying two apples," you can say, "Yes, I see a man buying two apples at the store," or "Yes, I see a man buying two red apples."

Intermediate and Advanced Fluency

Students can tell a story about their math facts with native-like fluency. Help them sound more like a book and use academic language by probing with statements such as, "Tell your story as if you were the teacher."

Summary

Not all homework or practice needs to be the same. Some students may reach 80 percent proficiency well before 24 practices. If so, they should move into extension activities. English language learners, however, are likely to need more than 24 practice sessions to be competent at a skill, so some of those practice sessions can be assigned as homework. It is important to be clear about the purpose of homework: practice, review, or preview. Keep in mind that it is OK for ELLs to review something they have already learned, and be mindful of giving them homework assignments they are able to understand.

9

REINFORCING EFFORT AND PROVIDING RECOGNITION

Classroom Instruction That Works indicates that reinforcing effort and providing recognition affect student attitudes and beliefs. Krashen and Terrell's "affective filter" hypothesis (1983) describes how negative feelings and lack of self-confidence and motivation can reduce a student's ability to acquire a new language. If a student suffers from low self-esteem, inadequate motivation, and apprehension, an affective filter goes up like an imaginary wall, seriously affecting the process of language acquisition.

Reinforcing Effort

Reinforcing effort is about helping students understand the relationship between effort and achievement. In order to improve student performance, we need to address their attitudes and beliefs about how they learn.

At the beginning of the year, I talked with the whole class about learning English. Even non-ELLs are in stages of language acquisition. Today we made a video and it was unbelievable. With my new ELLs, we had practiced and practiced and practiced the same song. They totally had it, so when the video was done, they said, "Oh! I can't believe I just did that!" Everybody came up to the ELLs saying, "You're doing a good job."

My class will not laugh if somebody says "tree" instead of "three." They are very positive with each other. By hearing "You can do it" from each other, I think it builds their effort up, and they want to do more. They are making every effort to use English, and if it's not perfect, it's OK, because the others are acknowledging that they're putting forth their best effort.

—D. H.

Generalizations from *Classroom Instruction That Works*

Two generalizations can be drawn from the research about reinforcing effort. First, students are unaware of the direct effect that effort has on success. Second, students can learn that the effort they put into a task has a direct effect on their success. Research shows that students who are taught about the connection between effort and achievement do better than students who are taught time-management techniques or comprehension strategies. In addition, a strong belief in effort increases motivation. ELLs and English-dominant students alike will benefit from learning to operate from a belief that effort pays off.

Classroom Recommendations

Classroom Instruction That Works makes two classroom recommendations related to reinforcing effort.

1. Explicitly teach students the importance of effort. This recommendation will benefit ELLs and English-dominant students alike. It involves telling students personal stories from your own life about times when effort led to success. You can also provide students with examples from the lives of well-known people (e.g., sports stars, historical figures, political leaders). If it is an Olympic year, remind students to pay attention to the "up-close and personal" stories of the athletes, which are loaded with examples of effort leading to achievement. One rarely hears athletes credit their success to luck.

Consider asking ELLs to share their language learning experiences. English-dominant students may not have any conception of what it takes to learn a second language.

2. Track effort and achievement. Students can use graphs or charts to see the correlation between effort and the progress of their achievement. Figure 9.1 depicts an effort rubric from *Classroom Instruction That Works*. Preproduction and Early Production students will benefit if the linguistic complexity of the chart in Figure 9.1 is reduced, as shown in Figure 9.2.

For mainstream students, you can use an achievement rubric like the one shown in Figure 9.3. Figure 9.4 depicts an achievement rubric adapted for ELLs. Depending on their language stage, students can either read the chart themselves or have the teacher or another student help them with it. Both ELLs and English-dominant students can use the effort and achievement chart in Figure 9.5.

Figure 9.1
Effort Rubric

4	I worked on the task until it was completed. I pushed myself to continue working on the task even when difficulties arose or a solution was not immediately evident. I viewed difficulties that arose as opportunities to strengthen my understanding.
3	I worked on the task until it was completed. I pushed myself to continue working on the task even when difficulties arose or a solution was not immediately evident.
2	I put some effort into the task, but I stopped working when difficulties arose.
1	I put very little effort into the task.

Source: Marzano, Pickering, and Pollock (2001), p. 52.

Figure 9.2
Effort Rubric Adapted for ELLs

4		I worked until I finished. I tried even when it was difficult. This lesson helped me learn more English.
3		I worked until I finished. I tried even when it was difficult.
2		I tried, but I stopped when it was too difficult.
1		I didn't try.

Figure 9.3
Achievement Rubric

4	I exceeded the objectives of the task or lesson.
3	I met the objectives of the task or lesson.
2	I met a few of the objectives of the task or lesson, but did not meet others.
1	I did not meet the objectives of the task or lesson.

Source: Marzano, Pickering, and Pollock (2001), p. 52.

Figure 9.4
Achievement Rubric Adapted for ELLs

4	I did more than learn the objective or lesson.
3	I learned the objective or lesson.
2	I did some things, but I didn't learn everything I needed to.
1	I did not learn what I needed to or do the lesson or activity.

Figure 9.5
Effort and Achievement Chart for All Students

Name:

Date	Assignment/ Activity/ Lesson	Effort Rubric	Achievement Rubric
Oct. 20	Homework— 5-paragraph essay	2	1
Oct. 25	Quiz	4	4

Below is a classroom example in which students tracked their levels of effort and resulting achievement. You will need to help ELLs by using strategies appropriate to their level of language acquisition. As always, keep in mind your tiered questions and the Word-MES formula.

Classroom Example

Subject: Physical Education
Content Objective: To understand the relationship between effort and achievement when running 100 meters.

For two weeks, students in Ms. Pickering's physical education class kept track of their level of effort using the rubric in Figure 9.6. They also tracked their times for running 100 meters. At the end of the two-week period, they discussed what they had learned about themselves.

Figure 9.6 Physical Education Effort Rubric	
4	I ran until I finished. I tried even when it was difficult.
3	I ran until I finished. I knew I couldn't do any better.
2	I tried, but I stopped when it was too difficult.
1	I didn't try.

Preproduction

Students will need your help understanding the effort rubric. You can use pantomime, gestures, and body language to aid understanding. Students can participate in the discussion by showing, pointing, or nodding.

Early Production

Students will initially need help understanding the effort chart as well, but they will then be able to complete effort and achievement charts independently. As for discussion, you will not hear whole sentences from them, but you can expect to hear key words. To include Early Production students in the discussion, plan to ask questions that require one- or two-word answers.

Speech Emergence

Students can complete their effort and achievement charts with little or no assistance. They are able to produce whole sentences and can be engaged in producing language to describe and report. Some question starters to draw these students into the discussion could include "What did you do when . . . ?" and "How did you react when . . . ?"

With kids who are learning a second language, you really need to cheerlead because otherwise they feel overwhelmed, and they feel that they aren't doing as well as the other kids. But you must also find a way that's intrinsically motivating for them, so that they aren't looking to you all the time. That is very difficult, and for each kid it's a little different. Some kids, especially in the beginning, end up really needing recognition, like one ELL who doesn't like to talk very much. I had to almost coerce it out of her, but now in small groups she is very expressive. She doesn't use two words when she knows six words that she can string together. So for some kids, it initially takes a lot more praise up front, but then you need to start weaning them once you see that they are there. I think that is a huge, huge task for any teacher.

—*E. B.*

Intermediate and Advanced Fluency
Students can independently complete the charts and participate in the discussion. Ask "why" questions to solicit their opinions, judgments, and creative replies.

Providing Recognition

Providing recognition involves giving students rewards or praise for accomplishments related to the attainment of a goal. Most of the strategies from *Classroom Instruction That Works* are cognitive, but providing recognition is an affective strategy because it deals with attitudes and beliefs. The research, however, shows that the effects of rewards and praise have been misunderstood.

Generalizations from *Classroom Instruction That Works*

The authors of *Classroom Instruction That Works* drew three generalizations from the research on providing recognition.

1. Rewards do not necessarily have a negative effect on intrinsic motivation. Although educators once thought that providing recognition decreased intrinsic motivation and did not improve student achievement, more recent research has proved otherwise.

2. Rewards are most effective when they are contingent upon the attainment of some standard of performance. Rewarding a student for simply completing a task can have a negative effect on motivation. You do not want to convey the message that students have to get paid off in order to accomplish something. Rewarding a student for reaching a specific performance goal, however, can have a positive effect and enhance intrinsic motivation.

Have you ever walked into a classroom and seen ELLs relegated to a corner and assigned to completing jigsaw puzzles while the rest of the class is engaged in academics? Rewarding ELLs for finishing jigsaw puzzles would undermine achievement and the students' perceptions of their abilities. Feel confident in the modifications you make for these students, as long as your expectations are high. ELLs will meet or exceed your expectations.

3. Abstract recognition (e.g., praise) is more effective in improving performance than are tangible rewards (e.g., candy, stickers). In fact, the more abstract and symbolic the reward, the more powerful a motivator it can be.

Verbal praise is one type of abstract recognition. Effective verbal praise specifies the particulars of the accomplishment. Preproduction and Early Production students will need to see and hear effective verbal praise. You can provide visual cues by pointing to what they accomplished or by adding pantomime, gestures, or body movement to verbal praise. Hearing you explain the details of their achievement will motivate higher-level ELLs.

Classroom Recommendations

Classroom Instruction That Works offers three recommendations for recognition in classroom practice.

1. Personalize recognition. A good time to do this is following the achievement of a specific performance goal. Because praise is most influential when attached to goal attainment, you are encouraged to ask students to identify the targets to be achieved.

Although ELLs may have different targets than English-dominant students, the ways in which you personalize recognition will be the same in many instances. If you choose to send letters home to parents when targets have been met, be sure to have them in a language the parents will understand (if possible).

2. Use the pause-prompt-praise strategy. This strategy is most effective when used with a student who is struggling with a particular task. The "pause" component of the strategy is implemented when the student is in the middle of a difficult task. Ask the student to stop for a moment. During this pause, talk about the difficulty the student is experiencing. During the "prompt" stage, you give the student specific suggestions on ways to improve performance. If the student's performance improves as a result of the pausing and prompting, you provide "praise."

The following scenario provides an example of how to implement the pause-prompt-praise strategy. An ELL was struggling with long division. His frustration must have been obvious, because the teacher stopped at his desk and asked him to put down his pencil. When the teacher saw that he was making mistakes mainly because his columns were sloppy, she gave him a piece of graph paper and showed him how to use it. He was surprised at how well it worked. The next time the teacher stopped at his desk, it was to congratulate him on having completed four problems with no mistakes.

3. Use concrete symbols of recognition. In addition to verbal acknowledgment, concrete symbols of recognition can include such items as awards, certificates, or coupons. These can be given for

I am a big fan of scratch-and-sniff stickers. I loved them when I was a kid, and that is my favorite thing as a teacher. I try to give them out for actions and accomplishments—not necessarily "You did a good job on this"; maybe it's more "You really took a risk," or "You really practiced this so you could read this to the class." I want to commend students for their effort in reaching a goal.

—E. B.

attaining a certain performance goal, but should not be provided for simply completing a task. These tokens of praise should not be offered as rewards per se, but simply as concrete symbols of recognition. Different students might enjoy different types of tokens. For ELLs, a happy face sticker can have more meaning than a written comment.

Adapting Personalized Recognition to the Stages of Language Acquisition

Let's examine how you can personalize recognition by praising ELLs for attainment in English language development. Let your ear be your guide when recognizing important milestones in language acquisition.

Preproduction
Students experience an important milestone when they move from being nonverbal to speaking in English.

Early Production
Students should be recognized for speaking in complete sentences.

Speech Emergence
Students deserve recognition for using expressions that are more linguistically complex.

Intermediate and Advanced Fluency
Students should be recognized for their growing repertoire of academic language.

Summary

Generalizations from the research tell us that rewards are most effective when tied to reaching a specific standard of performance. English language learners are always trying to accomplish two main goals: improvement of academic achievement and an increase in their English language proficiency. They need to be recognized for this double duty, as they not only have to learn new subject matter but also have to learn it in a new language.

Students should be recognized for progressing to a different stage of language acquisition. When it comes to personalizing recognition, there may not be anything more personal to an ELL than being recognized for becoming bilingual—a feat that perhaps only a small number in the school will accomplish.

10

GENERATING AND
TESTING HYPOTHESES

When we hear the phrase "generating and testing hypotheses," our minds jump to science; we think of laboratories, test tubes, and people in white coats. However, science does not have an exclusive claim on this instructional strategy, which engages students in complex reasoning that can be used in other content areas.

The process of generating and testing hypotheses requires ELLs to access prior knowledge, apply new knowledge, and explain their conclusions. Anytime we use "if-then" reasoning, we enter the realm of generating and testing hypotheses. (For example, when studying transportation, we might ask students what would happen if they had to travel by train rather than by car.)

Berman, Minicucci, McLaughlin, Nelson, and Woodworth (1995) wrote about the need to create new classroom environments that help ELLs acquire higher-level language and reasoning skills. They also note that these students do not always have full access to middle school science and math classes, where inductive and deductive reasoning are generally taught. With that in mind, it is particularly important not to wait for middle school science and mathematic classes to introduce students to inductive and deductive reasoning.

We had homophones a couple of weeks ago, which is horrible for 2nd grade ELLs. We made a flip chart with pictures for "plane" and "plain," and we acted them out. For "through" and "threw," we acted out going through a tunnel.

—*L. M.*

Generalizations from *Classroom Instruction That Works*

Classroom Instruction That Works suggests the following two generalizations about generating and testing hypotheses.

1. Hypothesis generation and testing can be approached in an inductive or deductive manner. When ELLs know how to apply the rules of English when writing, they are using deduction; when they read a passage and figure out the rules of the English language, they are using inductive reasoning.

2. Teachers must encourage students to explain their hypotheses and conclusions. Having students explain their hypotheses and conclusions presents an excellent opportunity for ELLs to develop oral and academic language. When students are explaining hyphotheses and conclusions, it is important to find time to facilitate English language development using the Word-MES formula.

Adapting the Generation and Testing of Hypotheses to the Stages of Language Acquisition

Preproduction
Students will need help with the vocabulary (word selection) involved in an explanation. By attaching pictures to key vocabulary and concepts, they will be able to point to items in the description.

These students will always need help learning multiple-meaning words. Attaching visual representations to words will help them learn and remember the differences, for example, between the word "fair" used as a noun (a carnival) and as an adjective (pale, light).

Early Production
You can help students by modeling correct English. Let's say you are engaging students in a historical investigation of George Washington and the cherry tree. If a student says, "He chopped (pronounced chop-ped)," you can model correct English by saying, "Yes, he chopped (pronounced correctly) down the cherry tree." Avoid overt corrections; repeat what the student said, but with correct pronunciation or grammar.

Speech Emergence
Students can benefit from having their language expanded. If a student says, "George Washington chopped down the cherry tree," you

can expand by adding an additional phrase: "Yes, George Washington chopped down the cherry tree with his hatchet."

Intermediate and Advanced Fluency

Students need language stimulation that will help them develop academic language. You can accomplish this by helping them sound like a book. Rephrase what they may have said and then add: "This is how the author of a book might say that."

Classroom Recommendations

Classroom Instruction That Works offers two classroom recommendations regarding hypotheses: Teachers should use a variety of tasks that emphasize generating and testing hypotheses, and they should require students to verbalize their hypotheses and conclusions. Tasks for generating and testing hypotheses include complex reasoning processes such as decision making, problem solving, invention, experimental inquiry, historical investigation, and systems analysis. ELLs can participate in generating and testing hypotheses in a mainstream classroom, but the language complexity must be reduced. For example, you may want to assign Preproduction students to any part of the process that requires hands-on activity. They should also be noting new vocabulary in notebooks and creating visuals to associate with the words. Early Production students will do well with manipulatives and opportunities that allow them to practice the vocabulary of the lesson. Speech Emergence students will understand the task at hand and will be able to communicate in short sentences. Intermediate and Advanced Fluency students will be participating at close to the same level as English-dominant students.

Classroom Example

Let's look at a mainstream lesson designed to help students understand inductive reasoning and then review how to adapt it for ELLs at various stages of language acquisition.

Subject: Social Studies
Content Objective: To learn that conclusions should be based on a number of observations.
   Tell students to take 5 to 10 minutes to go on an inductive outing. This means that you want them to walk around a designated area and carefully observe everything around them. Ask students to make

a list of several specific things that they observe. When they return to the room from a walk around the school grounds, ask them to write a conclusion that they can draw about the area—about the building, the grounds, or the people they have seen. Remind them to make sure their conclusions are supported by three or four observations.

Likewise, when students return to the classroom from a walk around the neighborhood, explain that they need to be ready to share the pieces of evidence that led to their conclusions. For example, if they noticed that a particular house had skis hanging in the garage, a basketball hoop above the driveway, tennis rackets on the porch, and a volleyball net in the backyard, they could reasonably conclude that the people living there are very involved in sports. Figure 10.1 presents a graphic organizer that you can use to help students understand what kind of information you are looking for.

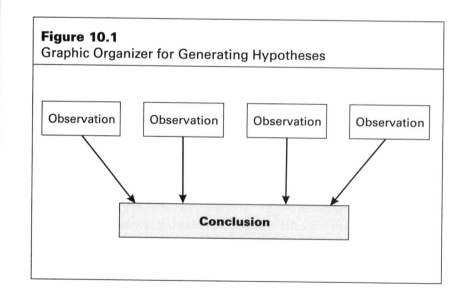

Figure 10.1
Graphic Organizer for Generating Hypotheses

Preproduction

Students can draw what they see. Upon returning to the classroom, you can help these students with word selection by giving them vocabulary for what they have represented in their pictures.

English language learners will need multiple encounters with words they are discovering in order to learn and remember the meaning of these new words. Encourage students to continue their language learning outside the classroom by developing a fun method for them to bring in evidence of seeing, hearing, or using identified vocabulary words outside of the school environment.

Early Production

Students can also use pictorial representations for what they've seen. When they return to the classroom, you can work with them on getting them to name what is in their pictures. This is a good time to model English; if an ELL says, "That a mower," the teacher correctly models, "Yes, that is a mower," but does not blatantly call attention to the grammatical error.

Speech Emergence

Students will be able to list what they observed and draw conclusions. Their writing will likely be composed of short, simple sentences, so they will benefit from you showing them how to expand their written language with adjectives and adverbs.

Intermediate and Advanced Fluency

Students will be able to write observations and conclusions. Help them "sound like a book" by asking them (as well as the English-dominant students) to write their conclusions as though they were detectives reporting on a news program.

The induction outing is a good way to introduce inductive reasoning to a class. You can use the strategies described in this chapter in any situation where students can make rich observations: on a field trip, during an assembly, when a movie is being shown, and so on. It is an experience that students enjoy, and it helps them to understand two important points about inductive reasoning: To discern patterns and connections, conclusions should be based on a number of observations; and conclusions that are based on inductive reasoning may or may not be accurate or true.

Preproduction and Early Production students should not be required to draw conclusions during the induction outing; they could work on vocabulary. Though there may be times when the language objective takes precedence over the content objective, this does not mean that ELLs are not learning or are not engaged in inductive reasoning. If you have ever been in a situation where you did not speak the language, you will know that you were constantly engaged in inductive reasoning as you were trying to figure out what was going on.

Summary

Generating and testing hypotheses is a strategy that emphasizes inductive and deductive reasoning. These two reasoning processes are usually reserved for particular classes at higher grade levels, but can be taught in the earlier grades using a variety of structured tasks.

To engage all ELLs in the process, you may need to reduce the linguistic complexity of the task. At other times, you will be paying close attention to how students are using their second language as they explain their hypotheses and conclusions.

Second language acquisition requires a significant amount of listening and speaking in order for the student to internalize the new language. Time set aside in the classroom for students to verbally explain hypotheses and conclusions will not only assist in the oral language development of ELLs, it will also help them develop academic content knowledge.

Sometimes, students' language needs will outweigh their academic needs, and you will have to develop their English language skills for the content-specific language demands. When you begin to focus on language learning in addition to content learning, you are helping your ELLs with what they need the most: an integration of language and content instruction.

11

IDENTIFYING SIMILARITIES AND DIFFERENCES

When we ask ELLs to identify similarities and differences, we give them the opportunity to learn content at a deeper level. In order to complete this task, students are required to activate prior knowledge, make new connections, construct meaning, and talk about their reasoning.

Generalizations from *Classroom Instruction That Works*

Classroom Instruction That Works identifies four generalizations from the research on identifying similarities and differences.

1. Teacher-directed activities deepen understanding for students and increase their ability to use knowledge. In teacher-directed activities, teachers provide a variety of explicit instruction regarding similarities and differences. Doing this allows students to better use the knowledge they are learning, because they will have received the knowledge linguistically and nonlinguistically.

During such an activity, you explain the steps and provide the information to be compared. When teaching ELLs how to identify similarities and differences, here are some tips that will facilitate student understanding:

- Represent what you say with visuals
- Use short, simple sentences with clear articulation
- Include gestures and facial expressions
- Use high-frequency vocabulary (and remember that nouns are better than pronouns)
- Reduce idiomatic expressions

The best advice given by mainstream teachers with ELLs in their classrooms is: When you think you have modeled enough, do it one more time!

2. Students should independently identify similarities and differences. Have students begin with a familiar topic, such as comparing school lunches over two days. Then, lead them into more content-related comparisons. This will help bridge the gap between teacher-directed and student-directed activities.

Preproduction students in particular will benefit from comparing familiar items because the familiar is here and now; it is laden with context and it forces us to use everyday vocabulary. Jim Cummins (1984) refers to this type of communication as "cognitively undemanding and context embedded" (p. 138). Context-embedded situations provide many clues for ELLs. The more talking opportunities that can take place in a meaningful communicative context (i.e., related to a student's background), the more successful the student will be.

As students move to unfamiliar contexts, they are pushed into using the vocabulary of academic English. Cummins (1984) calls this type of communication "cognitively demanding and context reduced" (p. 139). When students are asked to identify similarities and differences in order to gain insights, see distinctions, and change perspectives, the task becomes more academic in nature. Cummins notes that the reason many ELLs do not develop strong academic skills is because much of their initial instruction takes place in cognitively demanding, context-reduced situations that are inappropriate for the early stages of language acquisition.

3. When students represent similarities and differences in graphic or symbolic form, it enhances their ability to identify and understand similarities and differences. As we know from Chapter 4, accompanying verbal or written information with a visual representation helps ELLs make connections and construct meaning.

When we were working on similes and metaphors, it was hard for the ELLs to really compare and figure them out since some of it went right over their heads. So one thing I used was a picture describing the metaphor or simile: "His strength was like the towering mountains around him." So they drew what they thought would be somebody strong.

—Amy Libertini,
Berry Creek Middle School,
Edwards, Colorado

It's important to use familiar contexts. A lot of times I'll start with stories that [students] are familiar with. I think I've even done movies or things that fit more into pop culture because that is something that is motivating to them. We will do one as a group, and they kind of giggle, "Oh, I can't believe we are talking about Spiderman vs. Batman." It's something that they can really do, and it doesn't feel so academic, but they are learning the skill of identifying similarities and differences.

—E. B.

Representing similarities and differences in graphic or symbolic form should accompany both teacher-directed and student-directed activities. The advantage of having students use graphics and symbols is that they are required to use language to explain these nonlinguistic representations.

4. There are four different forms of identifying similarities and differences: comparing, classifying, creating analogies, and creating metaphors. Each of these forms is accompanied by language complexities that may need to be addressed and modified depending upon the student's stage of language acquisition. For example, Preproduction and Early Production students will do well with comparing two items according to various attributes (e.g., color, size, shape, function, composition, parts). Such an activity is appropriate at this level because it can involve pointing and one- or two-word responses. Speech Emergence students will do well with teacher-directed analogies as they fill in the blanks for relationships (e.g., "thermometer is to _____ as odometer is to _____"). Developing metaphors, however, requires sentences that express a student's ability to identify a general or basic pattern in a specific topic and then find another topic that is different but has the same general pattern. Students will need to be in the two final stages of language development before they can create student-directed metaphors.

Classroom Recommendations

Classroom Instruction That Works suggests five recommendations for identifying similarities and differences.

1. Remember to use different methods when asking students to identify similarities and differences. Many ELLs will benefit from orally identifying similarities and differences, whereas Intermediate, Advanced Fluency, and English-dominant students can engage in the same activity using written language.

2. Model each method of identifying similarities and differences. Provide visuals for ELLs while teaching them the steps of the task, use clear and concise speech with shorter sentences, and reduce your use of idioms while speaking.

3. Begin with a familiar topic when modeling. Using culturally familiar topics is one method of adapting a lesson for ELLs.

I always tell my ELLs that if you have an assignment, break it down into what's the same, what's different. If you just start writing, a lot of times it doesn't make as much sense, because your mind is going all different places. So if you organize your writing into a compare/contrast pattern before you write, it makes [things] a lot easier to understand. You have to really model this up front and then let them do it. Usually, I think this is something that kids—particularly second-language learners—can be successful with.

—E. B.

We were studying the ice men and mummies, so the students broke apart a cookie and pretended to be archaeologists. Some of the ELLs' comparisons were very literal, and some of them were very evaluative, so it was really good. The chocolate chip cookie was the bones, and that's why they were broken, and they did some great comparing with that. "Similarities and differences" is a strategy to understand things, but also a strategy to make sense of the new instruction coming in.

—E. S.

When I taught the students how to think about similarities and differences, we were studying the great migration of African Americans from the South to the North in the 1930s. I tried to relate that to something that my ELLs could relate to, which was immigration from Mexico. They found a lot of similarities and differences. That was good for the kids because the move from Mexico was such an important part of their lives and something that they are still dealing with on a daily basis as immigrants.

4. Use graphic organizers to represent the similarities and differences. Visual representations are always highly effective with ELLs. (See Chapter 4 for more on this topic.)

5. Guide ELLs through the process of identifying similarities and differences but lessen the support as you repeat activities.

Adapting Identification of Similarities and Differences to the Stages of Language Acquisition

Identifying similarities and differences has long been used in ESL classes to build basic vocabulary in different categories, including color words and words used to describe size (adjectives), shape words (nouns), and words for functions (verbs). This is done with an attribute chart (see Figure 11.1). The teacher gives a small group of students two objects, such as an apple and an orange, and then directs the students to the color box.

Figure 11.1
Attribute Chart

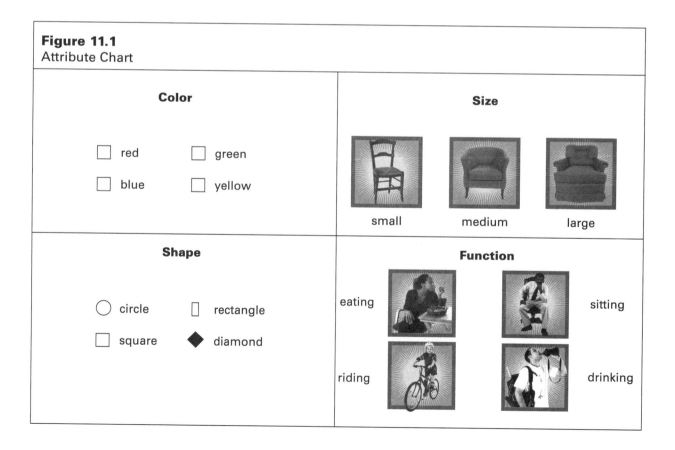

Preproduction

Students can point to the red color swatch when holding the apple and repeat the word "red."

Early Production

Students can complete a sentence starter with a one-word response: "The apple and the orange are the same because they are both . . . ."

Speech Emergence

Students can complete a sentence starter with a phrase or short sentence: "The apple and the orange are different because . . . ."

Intermediate and Advanced Fluency

Students will not need the sentence starters, but their responses will need some shaping. You should encourage them to "sound more like a book" by using words other than "same" and "different."

The attribute chart can be gradually increased to include more characteristics, such as the composition of items (what they are made of) and parts of the items (e.g., eraser and lead for a pencil). Plan for oral language development as students talk about what is the same and what is different. Attribute charts allow Preproduction students to build vocabulary, Early Production students to use familiar vocabulary, and Speech Emergence students to practice using sentences. Intermediate and Advanced Fluency students are able to work on improving their academic language knowledge by using words other than "same" and "different" as they compare items.

The next step is to allow students to select items to compare. This is a three-step process:

1. Select the items you want to compare.
2. Select the characteristics of the items on which you want to base your comparison.
3. Explain how the items are similar and different with respect to the characteristics you selected.

The process may be stated in simpler terms for young students:

1. What do I want to compare?
2. What is it about them that I want to compare?
3. How are they the same? How are they different?

Model the steps with a think-aloud: "First, I have to pick two things to compare. I want to compare an apple and an orange. Next, I have

We use similarities and differences a lot when we're analyzing literature and the motives of the authors and characters. We are constantly comparing and contrasting characters within a given selection or just one story compared to a different story. We use Venn diagrams or compare-and-contrast charts. That's what we do the most because our data show that it has the highest correlation [to improved academic achievement].

—W. G.

We do character analysis by talking about and writing similarities and differences. Besides comparing and contrasting two characters to each other, we also compare and contrast them to ourselves and our culture.

—Jolene Smith,
Kayenta Intermediate School,
Kayenta, Arizona

to pick the characteristics I'm going to compare. I want to compare color, shape, taste, and their parts. Finally, I describe how they are the same and different: The apple and the orange are the same because they are both round; the apple and the orange are different because the apple is red and the orange is orange."

After you have modeled the steps, make them available by posting them in the classroom. Students will have fun with this activity as they compare familiar objects from nonacademic topics.

It will not take long for students to become familiar with Venn diagrams (see Figure 11.2). Teachers can add another layer to the Venn diagram by having students select the characteristics of the items to be compared (Figure 11.3). ELLs can talk about similarities and differences, while English-dominant students write about the comparisons.

An additional level of complexity can be added by using a comparison matrix (see Figure 11.4). Initially, provide students with familiar items and tell them which characteristics to compare. Gradually, they can add to the list of characteristics (e.g., texture, how items are eaten, nutritional value).

Preproduction
Students are working to learn vocabulary and can be drawing pictures.

Early Production
Students are also working at an oral level using vocabulary. While you are circulating, be sure to model with sentence starters: "The apple, orange, and banana are the same/different because

_____ ."

Figure 11.2
Basic Venn Diagram

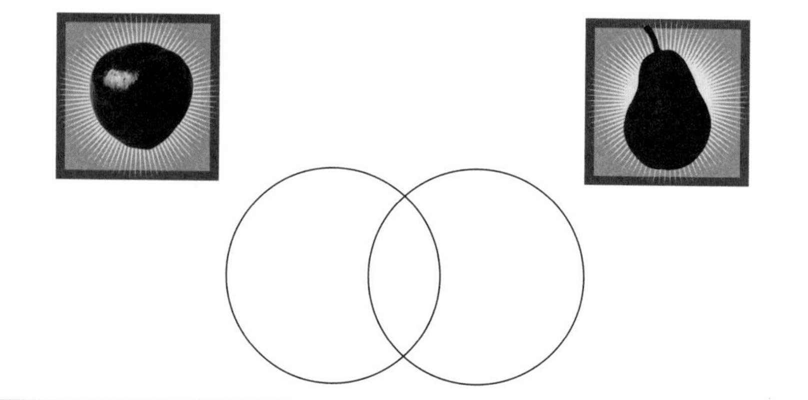

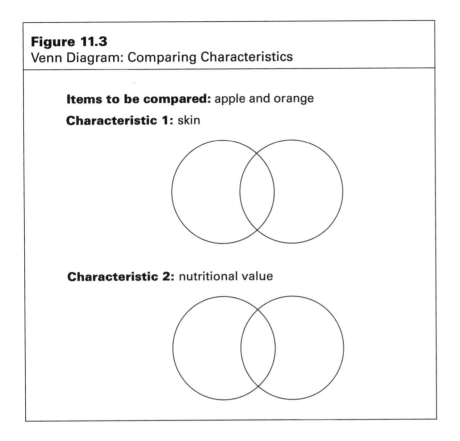

Figure 11.3
Venn Diagram: Comparing Characteristics

Items to be compared: apple and orange

Characteristic 1: skin

Characteristic 2: nutritional value

Speech Emergence
Students will rely less on sentence starters as they begin to produce longer sentences. As you listen, help these students by expanding the sentences, such as by turning short, disjointed sentences into compound sentences with conjunctions such as "and" and "because." These students can also be engaged in writing activities.

Intermediate and Advanced Fluency
Students can write about the similarities and differences they identify with the help of teacher feedback, as can English-dominant students.

Classroom Example

Figure 11.5 presents a real-life classroom example of an assignment dealing with similarities and differences. Figure 11.6 presents an example of a completed comparison matrix to go along with the activity. As you adapt the lesson for ELLs, you will want to focus on the Word-MES formula as discussed in Chapter 2.

Figure 11.4
Comparison Matrix

Characteristics	#1 Apple	#2 Orange	#3 Banana	Similarities and Differences
1. Color				
2. Size				
3. Shape				
4. Composition				

Preproduction
Students will be building vocabulary (word selection): *land, mountains, ocean,* color words, and words to describe size.

Early Production
Students will be using modeled sentence starters when talking about similarities and differences.

Speech Emergence
Students will be expanding their language as they talk and write.

Intermediate and Advanced Fluency
Students will begin to "sound like a book" as they write their comparisons.

Being able to describe a word according to its attributes is one of the first strategies ELLs will use in defining words. Next, they will provide examples of the word and then use synonyms. It is not until the later stages of language acquisition that they will define a word in the formal way that English-dominant students do—in terms of a larger class to which it belongs (i.e., defining "belt" as a clothing accessory or "dresser" as furniture).

Figure 11.5
"Stars or Starfish" Classroom Example

Subject: Science

Content Objective: To understand the composition and structure of the earth's atmosphere (e.g., temperature and pressure in different layers of the atmosphere, circulation of air masses).

Items you will be comparing: ocean, land, mountains

Characteristics to keep in mind: color, size, shape, sight, sound, and pressure

Starting point questions:

1. What do I want to compare?

2. What is it about them that I want to compare?

3. How are they the same? How are they different?

During our next unit, we will be learning about the deep, mysterious ocean. As we begin to understand the environment in the ocean, I'd like you to engage in an ongoing comparison. Using knowledge you acquired during our previous unit on the earth's atmosphere, identify the similarities and differences between what it would be like to go deeper and deeper into the ocean and what it would be like to go higher and higher to the top of a major mountain peak. Use characteristics for your comparison that highlight sights and sounds you would experience, but also be sure to demonstrate your understanding of the composition and structure of the earth's atmosphere.

Summary

Identifying similarities and differences allows ELLs rich opportunities to develop their second language. Teacher-directed activities are important as students become familiar with the tasks of comparing, classifying, creating metaphors, and creating analogies. Allow for plenty of talk time as students demonstrate verbal abilities before moving them into written forms of distinguishing similarities and differences.

Figure 11.6
Completed Comparison Matrix for "Stars or Starfish" Classroom Example

Characteristics	#1 Ocean	#2 Land	#3 Mountains	Similarities and Differences
1. Color	blue green	brown green gray	brown green purple	They share one same color, green.
2. Size	covers 2/3 of the earth	takes up a lot of space	tall	They are all different because the ocean covers more of the earth than land and the mountains are tall.
3. Sounds	waves	cars wind	wind	Land and mountains are the same because you can hear the wind from both of them. Ocean is different because you do not hear wind, you hear waves.
4. Pressure	more pressure as you go deeper	no more, no less	less pressure as you go higher	No similarities. Ocean and mountain are different because the pressure increases as you go lower and decreases as you go higher.

12

INVOLVING PARENTS
AND THE COMMUNITY

Numerous outside factors contribute to a student's potential for academic success. It is especially critical that school staff gather information from parents of ELLs about their backgrounds. Of particular importance are the students' native languages and cultures, the length and quality of prior formal education in their native language, any previous education they have received in U.S. schools, the amount of time they have been in the United States, and the extent of their exposure to English.

Knowing the native language and culture of students will help you tap into possible support resources for teaching these students in their native language. It will also reveal the educational customs and expectations of both the students and their parents. Remember that parents of recent immigrants may be unfamiliar with the U.S. education system. They may not know their rights, they may not understand what is expected of them, and they may not be familiar with academic concepts such as "standards-based education."

Information about a student's prior education in his native language can help you gauge the challenges the student will be facing. Students who arrive in U.S. schools with appropriate grade-level achievement in their native language will make the transition to learning in English more easily.

111

Parents whose children attended school consistently in their native country may have a very different perspective about education and parental involvement than mainstream U.S. parents. Homework policies and expectations for parental involvement may differ from those in their native country, for example.

You need to determine what exposure a student has had to the English language, even if he has lived in the United States for some time. A student's English could be very limited—even for a child who was born in the United States—if his family speaks only its native language at home and in the neighborhood.

Involving parents and the community is not just the teacher's job. School and district leadership teams need to develop comprehensive plans for parent and community involvement that include the parents of ELLs, as well as members of the community who share their ethnicity and language. Therefore, in addition to the model presented below, we provide an example of a plan to involve parents and the community from a district with a growing number of Spanish-speaking ELLs.

Epstein's Model of Parent and Community Involvement

A leading model of parent and community involvement was developed by Joyce Epstein at Johns Hopkins University (Epstein, Coates, Salinas, Sanders, & Simon, 1997). It is a research-based model that delineates six types of parent and community involvement. These types, and sample practices of each, are depicted in Figure 12.1.

How One District Engaged the Families of ELLs and Members of the Local Community

Mid-continent Research for Education and Learning (McREL) recently worked with the leadership team in a small rural district in Wyoming to engage the families of ELLs and members of the local community in the education process. This district had a growing population of Spanish-speaking students but very limited financial and human resources available to serve them.

The district's parent and community involvement work was conducted at two levels. First, McREL helped develop school staff capacity to work effectively with parents and families by helping district and school staff members learn more about the families of ELLs. Second, McREL helped to increase the knowledge and skills of the

Figure 12.1
Epstein's Six Types of Parent and Community Involvement

Type of Involvement	Sample Practices
Parenting Help all families establish home environments to support children as students.	• Parent education and other courses or training for parents (e.g., GED, college credit, family, literacy) • Family support programs to assist families with health, nutrition, and other services • Home visits at transition points to preschool and elementary, middle, and high school
Communicating Design effective forms of school-to-home and home-to-school communications about school programs and children's progress.	• Conferences with every parent at least once a year • Language translators to assist parents as needed • Regular schedule of useful notices, memos, phone calls, newsletters, and other communications
Volunteering Recruit and organize parent help and support.	• School and classroom volunteer program to help teachers, administrators, students, and other parents • Parent room or family center for volunteer work, meetings, and resources for families • Annual postcard survey to identify all available talents, times, and locations of volunteers
Learning at Home Provide information and ideas to families about how to help students at home with homework and other curriculum-related activities, decisions, and planning.	• Information for families on skills required for students in all subjects at each grade • Information on homework policies and how to monitor and discuss schoolwork at home • Family participation in setting student goals each year and in planning for college or work
Decision Making Include parents in school decisions and in the development of parent leaders and representatives.	• Active PTA/PTO or other parent organizations, advisory councils, or committees for parent leadership and participation • Independent advocacy groups to lobby and work for school reform and improvements • Networks to link all families with parent representatives
Collaborating with Community Identify and integrate resources and services from the community to strengthen school programs, family practices, and student learning and development.	• Information for students and families on community health; cultural, recreational, or social support; and other programs or services • Information on community activities that are linked to learning skills and talents, including summer programs for students • Service to the community by students, families, and schools (e.g., recycling, art, music, drama, and other activities for seniors or others)

Source: Adapted from Epstein, Coates, Salinas, Sanders, and Simon (1997).

parents and families so that they could actively participate in school activities and their children's education.

District Activities

Assessing parent and family needs. The district leadership team needed to know what families in the community wanted to learn. To get to know the community, the school staff gathered information about the parents and families of ELLs at a parent meeting at the beginning of the school year using two Spanish-language questionnaires.

One questionnaire was designed to gather basic information, such as where the family was from originally, how long they had lived in the United States (and in the local area), and what academic expectations the parents had for their children. The other questionnaire was designed to determine what the parents knew about school systems in the United States. It measured the extent of their knowledge on topics such as No Child Left Behind (NCLB) and standards-based education and whether they had previously had opportunities to learn how to communicate with their children's teachers and help their children with assignments. Staff used the results of both questionnaires to outline the content of parent meetings for the rest of the year.

Developing parents' understanding. After completing the needs assessment, McREL took a number of steps to ensure parent participation. Intensive outreach was conducted: Flyers were sent home and follow-up phone calls were made (both in Spanish) to ensure that a reasonable number of parents participated in scheduled meetings. McREL staff conducted monthly on-site family meetings, with all training and activities conducted in Spanish.

To develop the necessary knowledge and skills to help their children, parents are encouraged to actively participate in the decision-making aspect of schooling. To aid in this area, McREL offered training on the following topics:

- **Parent rights and responsibilities under NCLB.** Parents learned that they can expect to have their children taught by a highly qualified teacher, become proficient in English while learning academic content, and be tested annually for their English language proficiency. Parents can expect to know if their children have been identified and recommended for placement in an ESL program and learned that they have the right to accept or refuse these services. They can also expect to receive information on their children's performance on tests of academic achievement.

- **Standards-based education.** Staff shared the Wyoming standards for language development with parents. Parents learned that their children's proficiency in personal, social, and academic uses of English would be expected to increase with these standards.
- **Communicating effectively at parent–teacher conferences.** McREL based its training on this topic on Southwest Educational Development Laboratory's (2003) advice for parents on preparing and participating actively in parent–teacher conferences. Parents were encouraged to ask the teacher what strategies will be used to help their children gain knowledge and skills in content areas, how their children's performance will be assessed, and what they can do at home to help their children learn. Parents were also advised to plan a follow-up conference with the teacher to stay abreast of their children's progress.
- **Availability of ESL classes and other services in the community.** The district formed a partnership with the local community college, whereby college staff attended a parent meeting and invited the adults to attend ESL classes in the evening. The teachers of the ESL classes distributed brochures explaining the courses and indicating the community centers where they would be held. At the end of the year, the college's ESL teachers presented the parents with awards for hours of coursework completed. Parents also learned about additional community resources, such as summer reading programs at the library, year-round activities at the town recreation center, summer school, community agencies that assist with health issues, and summer employment opportunities for teens.

Encouraging parent involvement. Parents from other cultures may view their role in their children's education differently than U.S. parents. For example, instead of asking their children questions about a story—asking them to predict the outcome, for instance, or having them interpret the story based on their own experiences—immigrant parents from rural areas of Mexico and Central America are more likely to use the story to teach a moral lesson (Valdes, 1996).

To help the parents in the Wyoming district contribute more actively to the education of their children, McREL offered training at the monthly meetings on increasing the knowledge and skills parents need to help their children with the acquisition of English, literacy development, and academic proficiency in different content areas. McREL also offered training on increasing the knowledge and skills parents need to effectively collaborate with their children's teachers, specialists, and paraprofessionals.

Three-Year Parent and Community Involvement Plan

See Appendix C for an example of a three-year parent and community involvement plan, based on the experience of the Wyoming district.

Recommendations

Based on the experience in the Wyoming school district we examined, we offer the following recommendations to help schools involve parents and the community in the educational process.

Begin with the school itself. Make it evident through visuals that different languages and cultures are represented in the school. Visuals could include signs that say "Welcome" or "Visitors Must Check in at the Office" in another language, as well as artwork representing another culture (or cultures). Reallocate library resources for buying books that are written in other languages and represent various cultures. Use other financial resources to purchase classroom materials that will broaden all students' understanding of different cultures.

Use bilingual staff to the extent possible. If bilingual staff members are available in the district, use some of the approaches and ideas discussed earlier in this chapter to guide their training and work with the parents of ELLs. It is important to note that bilingual paraprofessionals are exempt from NCLB's "highly qualified" requirements if they work solely as translators or on parental involvement issues.

Involve the community. Besides involving the parents, it is important to search out other community members who share the same native language as the newcomers. Include them in all plans for building not only a family–school partnership but also a family- community-school network.

Hold regular meetings. Hold monthly or bimonthly meetings to inform parents how they can participate in decision making at their children's schools, along with other ways they can contribute to their children's education. Be sure to extend the invitation often and in several ways. During meetings, actively engage parents by having the facilitator check for understanding, ask for personal stories, and ask what else they would like to learn.

Offer ESL classes for parents. Districts can form partnerships with community colleges and other agencies to offer ESL classes to the parents of ELLs.

Summary

The unique qualities of ELLs and their families justify the need for modifying approaches typically used to involve parents in the school culture. A three-year comprehensive plan can be advantageous when planning for parent and community involvement, as it broadens a leadership team's knowledge of various types of participation.

CONCLUSION

As we noted in the Introduction, the number of ELLs in the United States has skyrocketed. For the most part, mainstream teachers are now responsible for helping these students learn English and master required academic content. Are teachers prepared, however, to meet the needs of this special population?

Available data indicate that, for the most part, few mainstream teachers are prepared to work with ELLs. The 1999–2000 *Schools and Staffing Survey* by the U.S. Department of Education (n.d.) indicated that of the 41.2 percent of teachers who taught ELLs, only 12.5 percent had had eight or more hours of training to do so in the last three years.

One of the authors of this book, Kathleen Flynn, vividly remembers her early days as a substitute teacher in an urban school district, where she was frequently placed in a mainstream classroom that included many ELLs. As a novice teacher, she was still learning how to teach English-dominant students and had received no training in how to modify teaching strategies for ELLs. It was a lose-lose situation—a day in the classroom wasted for the ELLs, and a day of frustration for Kathleen. She did her best, but inevitably she would leave at the end of the school day knowing she had not been successful in reaching the ELLs.

We wrote this book with Kathleen's experience fresh in our minds, hoping that it will help you turn your lessons into win-win situations for both you and your ELL students. You and all of the students in your classroom deserve days filled with rich learning experiences where you, as the teacher, feel confident that you have modified and adapted your teaching strategies in ways that have allowed your students to experience success in the classroom and beyond.

APPENDIX A

TYPES OF GRAPHIC ORGANIZERS

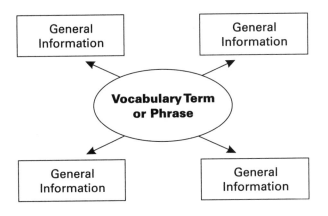

| General Information | | General Information |

Vocabulary Term or Phrase

| General Information | | General Information |

Vocabulary Terms and Phrases

Provides the most important characteristics of a term or phrase, along with examples that further describe it. Students need to have enough information to describe the term or phrase accurately and should have no misconceptions about its meaning, though they may have only surface-level understanding.

Event / Event / Event / Event / Event / Event

Time Sequence

Includes a chronology of important events that occurred between two points in time. (Example: The events that occurred between the moment of John F. Kennedy's assassination on November 22, 1963, and his burial on November 25.)

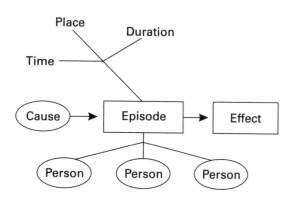

Episodes

Used for events that occurred at a specific time and place, had specific participants, lasted for a specific duration of time, involved a specific sequence of events, were caused by specific events, and had specific effects. (Example: The events of the Watergate burglary and its effects on the presidency of Richard M. Nixon.)

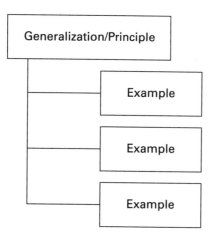

Generalizations/Principles

Generalizations are statements for which examples can be provided. (Example: "U.S. presidents often come from families of great wealth or influence.") Principles are specific types of generalizations that deal with relationships. Cause/effect principles articulate causal relationships (e.g., "Tuberculosis is caused by the tubercle bacillus"), whereas correlational principles describe relationships that are not necessarily causal but in which a change in one factor is associated with a change in another factor (e.g., "The increase in lung cancer among women is directly proportional to the increase in the number of women who smoke").

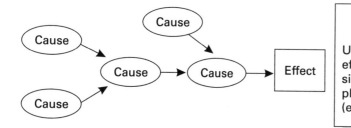

Cause/Effect Sequence

Used for events that produce a product or an effect. Causes may range from simple and singular (e.g., a game being lost because a player dropped the ball) to complex networks (e.g., the events leading up to the U.S. Civil War).

APPENDIX B

TYPES OF SUMMARY FRAMES

The Narrative Frame

The *narrative* or *story* frame commonly contains the following elements:

- **Characters:** the characteristics of the main characters in the story
- **Setting:** the time, place, and context in which the information took place
- **Initiating event:** the event that starts the action rolling in the story
- **Internal response:** how the main characters react emotionally to the initiating event
- **Goal:** what the main characters decide to do as a reaction to the initiating event
- **Consequence:** how the main characters try to accomplish the goal
- **Resolution:** how the goal turns out

Components 3–7 are sometimes repeated to create what is called an *episode*.

Frame Questions

- Who are the main characters in the story?
- When and where did the story take place? What was the place like?
- What happened at the start of the story?
- How did the main characters react to that event?
- As a result of what happened, what did the main characters decide to do? Did they set a goal? What was it?
- What did the main characters do to try to accomplish their goal?
- How did things turn out?

The Topic-Restriction-Illustration Frame

The *topic, restriction,* and *illustration* (T-R-I) pattern is commonly found in expository material:

- **Topic (T):** general statement about the information to be discussed
- **Restriction (R):** statement that limits the information in some way
- **Illustration (I):** example of the topic or restriction

Here's an example:

- T: In 1981, the Braves were the best team in baseball.
- R: Their pitching staff was excellent.
- I: Larry Hutchins was 20–2 for the season.
- I: Bob Ewy had the fastest pitch in the majors.
- R: Their hitters were also excellent.
- I: Dave Wallace batted .421.
- I: Walter Zebleman hit 42 homers.

As the example illustrates, the T-R-I frame can have a number of restrictions and accompanying illustrations.

Frame Questions

- T: What is this story about in general?
- R: What information does the author give that narrows or restricts the general topic?
- I: Wha t examples does the author present to illustrate the restriction?

The Argumentation Frame

Argumentation patterns attempt to support a claim. They contain the following elements:

- **Evidence:** information that leads to a claim (e.g., streets filled with violence)
- **Claim:** the assertion that something is true (e.g., "Our city is becoming a haven for crime")
- **Support:** examples of or explanations for the claim (e.g., "Violent offenders infest our judicial system" [example]; "The violence is a result of poor city management" [explanation])
- **Qualifier:** a restriction on the claim or evidence counter to the claim (e.g., "However, there is a ray of hope")

Frame Questions

- What information does the author present that leads her to make a claim?
- What claim does the author make about a problem or situation? What does she assert is so?
- What examples or explanations does the author present to support her claim?
- Does the author present a restriction on the claim?

The Problem-Solution Frame

Problem-solution patterns introduce a problem and then identify one or more solutions to the problem:

- **Problem:** There will soon be a worldwide oil shortage.
- **Solution:** One solution might be the development of solar energy.
- **Solution:** Another solution could be to conserve energy by using it less.
- **Solution:** Finally, a tactic might be to replace gasoline with ethanol-based fuel.

Frame Questions

- What is the problem?
- What is a possible solution?
- What is another possible solution?
- What is yet another possible solution?

The Conversation Frame

A *conversation* is a verbal interchange among two or more people. Conversations commonly have the following components:

- **Greeting:** some acknowledgment that the parties have not seen each other for a while
- **Inquiry:** a question about some general or specific topic
- **Discussion:** an elaboration or analysis of the topic; commonly included in the discussion are the following:
  - *Assertions:* statements of facts by the speaker
  - *Requests:* statements that solicit actions from the listener
  - *Promises:* statements that assert that the speaker will perform certain actions
  - *Demands:* statements that identify specific actions to be taken by the listener
  - *Threats:* statements that specify consequences to the listener if commands are not followed
  - *Congratulations:* statements that indicate the value the speaker puts on something done by the listener

Frame Questions

- What question or topic was brought up?
- How did the discussion progress? What facts were stated?
- What did the characters say to each other to begin the conversation?
  - Did either person make a request of the other?
  - Did either person demand a specific action from the other?
  - Did either person threaten specific consequences if a demand was not met?
  - Did either person say something that indicated that he or she valued something that the other had done?

APPENDIX C

EXAMPLE OF A THREE-YEAR PARENT AND COMMUNITY INVOLVEMENT PLAN

September 2005 to June 2008

VISION: A COMPREHENSIVE PROGRAM OF SIX TYPES OF INVOLVEMENT

Outline the activities that might help your school improve all six types of involvement over the next three years. What steps might your Action Team take in Year 1, Year 2, and Year 3 to improve Parenting, Communicating, Volunteering, Learning at Home, Decision Making, and Collaborating with the Community? (Use this form *after* completing "Starting Points: An Inventory of Present Practices" and *before* completing the One-Year Action Plan—Form A.)

Source: Epstein, J. L., Coates, L., Salinas, K. C., Sanders, M. G., & Simon, B. S. (1997). *School, family, and community partnerships: Your handbook for action* (pp. 126–128, 130–135). Thousand Oaks, CA: Corwin Press. Reprinted by permission.

Type 1: Parenting

Assist families with parenting skills, family support, understanding child and adolescent development, and setting home conditions to support learning at each age and grade level. Obtain information from families to help schools understand children's strengths, talents, and needs, and families' backgrounds, cultures, and goals for their children.

Vision: What is your Action Team's broad goal for improving Type 1: Parenting over the next three years? *Parents learning English. Partner with outreach organizations. Same level of opportunities; for example, Booster Club. See more Hispanic parents involved.*

Which activities might you conduct over three years to reach your vision for Type 1: Parenting?

Year 1. *District leads parent meetings. Parents have opportunities to share concerns; for example, "Who do I call when child has missed the bus?" Home visits. Encourage parents to use primary language at home—be intentional at a meeting.*

Year 2. *Establish lines of communication between school district and community outreach organizations.*

Year 3. *Pair Hispanic family with non-Hispanic family. Invite parents to attend events and meetings so they do not have to attend alone. Invite parents to Booster club.*

Type 2: Communicating

Communicate with families about school programs and student progress using school-to-home and home-to-school communications. Create two-way channels so that families can easily contact teachers and administrators.

Vision: What is your Action Team's broad goal for improving Type 2: Communicating over the next three years? *School-to-home and home-to-school communications. Continue to employ Spanish-speaking paraprofessionals. Continue to translate communications.*

Which activities might you conduct over three years to reach your vision for Type 2: Communicating?

Year 1. *Home visits. Mid-term phone calls. School newsletters discussed with high school students.*

Year 2. *Report on positive student behaviors. Inform parents of behavioral concerns. Don't overlook either because of language differences.*

Year 3. *Communicate to parents students' decisions about classes at the high school level.*

Type 3: Volunteering

Improve recruitment, training, activities, and schedules to involve families as volunteers and audiences at the school or in other locations to support students and the school's programs.

Vision: What is your Action Team's broad goal for improving Type 3: Volunteering over the next three years? *Increase frequency, numbers, and variety/types of volunteering in schools.*

Which activities might you conduct over three years to reach your vision for Type 3: Volunteering?

Year 1. *Group training for parents who may be interested in volunteering for "teacher help" in areas such as craft preparation, and so forth.*

Year 2. *Some type of recognition for the volunteers at a Parent Night. Parents can be recognized for giving time to attend student performances, games, assemblies, celebrations, and other events.*

Year 3. *Parents help collect tickets and hand out programs for student performances or games. Contact parents to remind them of student performances, games, assemblies, celebrations, and other events.*

Type 4: Learning at Home

Involve families with their children in academic learning activities at home including homework, goal setting, and other curriculum-related activities and decisions.

Vision: What is your Action Team's broad goal for improving Type 4: Learning at Home over the next three years? *Get information out to parents of ELLs and students about curriculum, school-related activities, and ideas for better involvement of the parents at those activities.*

Which activities might you conduct over three years to reach your vision for Type 4: Learning at Home?

Year 1. Technology workshop to help parents access Infinite Campus (and having it appear in Spanish).

Year 2. Continuation of summer learning for ELL students.

Year 3. Formal communication about student homework. Interactive homework that requires students to talk with someone about something they are learning in class.

Type 5: Decision Making

Include families as participants in school decisions, governance, and advocacy activities through PTA/PTO, committees, councils, and other parent organizations. Assist family representatives to obtain information from and give information to those they represent.

Vision: What is your Action Team's broad goal for improving Type 5: Decision Making over the next three years? *Get parents of ELLs more involved in the school decision-making process.*

Which activities might you conduct over three years to reach your vision for Type 5: Decision Making?

Year 1. Electing/appointing a liaison/representative for each school's PTO for better input from parents of ELLs for school needs.

Year 2. More education about the history and products of school PTOs.

Year 3. Generate a list of parents of ELLs willing to attend PTO.

Type 6: Collaborating with the Community

Coordinate the work and resources of community businesses, agencies, cultural and civic organizations, and other groups to strengthen school programs, family practices, and student learning and development. Enable students, staff, and families to contribute services to the community.

Vision: What is your Action Team's broad goal for improving Type 6: Collaborating with the Community over the next three years? *To increase awareness of parents as to what cultural and educational resources are available in this community.*

Which activities might you conduct over three years to reach your vision for Type 6: Collaborating with the Community?

Year 1. *Contact the recreation center about what community services are already in place for Hispanics. Does anyone speak Spanish?*

Year 2. *Collaborate with the community college ESL instructor to see what community information packets are available.*

Year 3. *Strengthen relationship between district and college ESL program. Is there a Spanish social service program guide available?*

REFERENCES

Alanis, I. (2004). Effective instruction: Integrating language and literacy. In
C. Salinas (Ed.), *Scholars in the field: The challenge of migrant education* (pp.
211–224). Charleston, WV: Appalachian Regional Education Laboratory.

Anderson, J. R. (1995). *Learning and memory: An integrated approach*. New York:
Wiley and Sons.

Asher, J. (1977). *Learning another language through actions: The complete teacher's
guide*. Los Gatos, CA: Sky Oaks Publications.

Beck, I. L., McKeown, M. G., & Kucan, L. (2002). *Bringing words to life: Robust
vocabulary instruction*. New York: Guildford Press.

Berman, P., Minicucci, C., McLaughlin, B., Nelson, B., & Woodworth, K.
(1995). *School reform and student diversity: Case studies of exemplary practices
for LEP students*. Washington, DC: National Clearinghouse for English
Language Acquisition.

Brinton, D., Snow, M., & Wesche, M. (1989). *Content-based second language
instruction*. Boston: Heinle and Heinle.

Brophe, J., & Good, T. (1986). Teacher behavior and student achievement. In
M. Wittrock (Ed.), *Handbook of research on teaching* (pp. 328–375). New
York: Macmillan.

Brown, H. D. (2000). *Principles of language learning and teaching*. New York:
Addison Wesley Longman, Inc.

Carlo, M. S., August, D., McLaughlin, B., Snow, C. E., Dressler, C., Lippman,
D. N., Lively, T. J., & White, C. E. (2004). Closing the gap: Addressing the
vocabulary needs of English-language learners in bilingual and mainstream

classrooms. *Reading Research Quarterly, 39,* 188–215.

Chamot, A. U., & O'Malley, M. (1994). *The CALLA handbook: Implementing Cognitive Academic Language Learning Approach.* Reading, MA: Addison-Wesley.

Cochran, C. (1989). Strategies for involving LEP students in the all-English-medium classroom: A cooperative learning approach. *NCELA Program Information Guide Series* (No. 12).

Coleman, J. S., Campbell, E., Hobson, C., McPartland, J., Mood, A., Weinfeld, F., & York, R. (1966). *Equality of educational opportunity.* Washington, DC: U.S. Government Printing Office.

Collier, V. P., & Thomas, W. P. (1989). How quickly can immigrants become proficient in school English? *Journal of Educational Issues of Language Minority Students, 5,* 26–38.

Crandall, J., Spanos, G., Christian, D., Simich-Dudgeon, C., & Willetts, K. (1987). Integrating language and content instruction for language minority students. *Teacher Resource Guide Series* (No. 4). Washington, DC: Office of Bilingual Education and Minority Language Affairs. (ERIC Document Reproduction Service No. ED 291 247).

Cummins, J. (1984). *Bilingualism and special education: Issues in assessment and pedagogy.* San Diego, CA: College-Hill Press.

Dong, Y. R. (2004/2005). Getting at the content. *Educational Leadership, 62,* 14–19.

Earle-Carline, S. (n.d.). *Providing language feedback.* Retrieved April 22, 2005, from www.ncela.gwu.edu/oela/summit/Language_Feedback.

Echevarria, J., & Graves, A. (1998). *Sheltered content instruction: Teaching English language learners with diverse abilities.* Needham Heights, MA: Allyn and Bacon.

Echevarria, J., Vogt, M., & Short, D. J. (2000). *Making content comprehensible for English language learners: The SIOP model.* Needham Heights, MA: Allyn and Bacon.

Education Market Research Corner Archives. (2004, December). ELL market: National market overview. *The Complete K–12 Newsletter.*

Englander, K. (2002, February). Real life problem solving: A collaborative learning activity. *English Teaching Forum,* 8–11.

Epstein, J. L., Coates, L., Salinas, K. C., Sanders, M. G., & Simon, B. S. (1997). *School, family, and community partnerships: Your handbook for action.* Thousand Oaks, CA: Corwin Press.

Fashola, O. S., Slavin, R. E., Calderón, M., & Durán, R. (1997). *Effective programs for Latino students in elementary and middle schools.* Paper prepared for the Hispanic Dropout Project, Office of Educational Research and Improvement, U.S. Department of Education, Washington, DC.

Fathman, A. K., Quinn, M. E., & Kessler, C. (1992). Teaching science to English learners, grades 4–8. *NCELA Program Information Guide Series* (No. 11), 1–27.

Fraser, B. J., Walberg, H. J., Welch, W. W., & Hattie, J. A. (1987). Synthesis of educational productivity research. *Journal of Educational Research, 11*(2), 145–252.

Garcia, E., & Pearson, P. D. (1991). Modifying reading instruction to maximize its effectiveness for "all" students. In M. S. Knapp & P. M. Shields (Eds.), *Better schooling for the children of poverty: Alternatives to conventional wisdom* (pp. 31–60). Berkeley, CA: McCutchan.

Genesee, F. (1994). Integrating language and content: Lessons from immersion. *Educational Practice Reports* (No. 11). Washington, DC: Center for Applied Linguistics.

Gibbons, P. (1991). *Learning to learn in a second language.* Portsmouth, NH: Heinemann.

Herrell, A., & Jordan, M. (2004). *Fifty strategies for teaching English language learners.* Upper Saddle River, NJ: Pearson Education, Inc.

Hodgkinson, H. L. (2003). *Leaving too many children behind: A demographer's view on the neglect of America's youngest children.* Washington, DC: Institute for Educational Leadership.

Jencks, C., Smith, M. S., Ackland, H., Bane, J. J., Cohen, D., Grintlis, H., Heynes, B., & Michelson, S. (1972). *Inequality: A reassessment of the effects of family and schools in America.* New York: BasicBooks.

Johnson, D. W., & Johnson, R. T. (1999). *Learning together and alone: Cooperative, competitive, and individualistic learning.* Boston: Allyn and Bacon.

Kagan, S. (1995). We can talk: Cooperative learning in the elementary ESL classroom. (ERIC Document Reproduction Service No. ED 382 035).

Kagan, S., & McGroarty, M. (1993). Principles of cooperative learning for language and content gains. In D. Holt (Ed.), *Cooperative learning: A response to linguistic and cultural diversity* (pp. 47–66). McHenry, IL: Delta Systems.

Krashen, S. D., & Terrell, T. (1983). *The natural approach: Language acquisition in the classroom.* Oxford: Pergamon.

Lou, Y., Abrami, P. C., Spence, J. C., Paulsen, C., Chambers, B., & d'Apollonio, S. (1996). Within-class grouping: A meta-analysis. *Review of Educational Research, 66*(4), 423–458.

Marzano, R. J. (2004). *Building background knowledge for academic achievement.* Alexandria, VA: Association for Supervision and Curriculum Development.

Marzano, R. J., Norford, J. S., Paynter, D. E., Pickering, D. J., & Gaddy, B. (2001). *A handbook for classroom instruction that works.* Alexandria, VA: Association for Supervision and Curriculum Development.

Marzano, R. J., Pickering, D. J., & Pollock, J. E. (2001). *Classroom instruction that works.* Alexandria, VA: Association for Supervision and Curriculum Development.

McLaughlin, B., August, D., Snow, C., Carlo, M., Dressler, C., White, C., Lively, T., & Lippman, D. (2000, April). *Vocabulary improvement and reading in English language learners: An intervention study.* Paper presented at a research symposium of the Office of Bilingual Education and Minority Language Affairs, U.S. Department of Education, Washington, DC.

Mohan, B. (1990). Integration of language and content. In *Proceedings of the first research symposium on limited English proficient students' issues* (pp. 113–160). Washington, DC: U.S. Department of Education, Office of Bilingual Education and Minority Languages Affairs.

National Clearinghouse for English Language Acquisition. (n.d.a). *Frequently asked questions.* Retrieved April 25, 2005, from www.ncela.gwu.edu/expert/faq/14shortage.html.

National Clearinghouse for English Language Acquisition. (n.d.b). *In the classroom: A toolkit for effective instruction of English learners.* Retrieved June 20, 2005, from www.ncela.gwu.edu/practice/itc/lessons/schcomprehensible.html.

National Clearinghouse for English Language Acquisition. (n.d.c). *In the classroom: Guiding practices.* Retrieved June 10, 2005, from www.ncela.gwu.edu/practice/itc/info/comprehensible_i.html.

Newell, A., & Rosenbloom, P. S. (1981). Mechanisms of skill acquisition and the law of practice. In J. R. Anderson (Ed.), *Cognitive skills and their acquisition.* Hillsdale, NJ: Erlbaum and Associates.

Ogle, D. (1986, February). The K-W-L: A teaching model that develops active reading of expository text. *The Reading Teacher, 39,* 564–570.

Ogle, D. M. (1989). The "know, want to know" learning strategy. In K. D. Muth (Ed.), *Children's comprehension of text* (pp. 205–223). Newark, DE: International Reading Association.

Oliver, R. (2003). Interactional context and feedback in child ESL classrooms. *Modern Language Journal, 87,* 519–533.

Ovando, C. J., Collier, V. P., & Combs, M. C. (2003). *Bilingual and ESL classrooms.* New York: McGraw-Hill.

Padrón, Y. N. (1992). The effect of strategy instruction on bilingual students' cognitive strategy use in reading. *Bilingual Research Journal, 16,* 35–51.

Palincsar, A. S., & Brown, A. L. (1984, Spring). Reciprocal teaching of comprehension-fostering and comprehension-monitoring activities. *Cognitive Instruction, 2,* 167–175.

Paynter, D., Bodrova, E., & Doty, J. K. (2005). *For the love of words: Vocabulary instruction that works.* San Francisco, CA: Jossey-Bass.

Ramirez, J. D. (1992). Executive summary of the final report: Longitudinal study of structured English immersion strategy, early-exit and late-exit transitional bilingual education programs for language minority children. *Bilingual Research Journal, 16,* 1–62.

Robinson, F. (1961). *Effective study.* New York: Harper and Row.

Sanders, W. L., & Horn, S. P. (1994). The Tennessee value-added assessment system (TVAAS): Mixed-model methodology in educational assessment. *Journal of Personnel Evaluation in Education, 8,* 299–311.

Schoen, F., & Schoen, A. A. (2003). Action research in the classroom. *Teaching Exceptional Children, 35,* 16–21.

Segal, B. (1983). *Teaching English through action.* Brea, CA: Berty Segal, Inc.

Short, D. (1991). Integrating language and content instruction: Strategies and techniques. *NCELA Program Information Guide Series* (No. 7), 1–23.

Short, D. J. (1994). Study examines role of academic language in social studies content-ESL classes. *Forum, 17*(3).

Simich-Dudgeon, C. (1998). Classroom strategies for encouraging collaborative discussion. *Directions in Language and Education, 12,* 1–14.

Simich-Dudgeon, C., McCreedy, L., & Schleppegrell, M. (1988). *Helping limited English proficient children communicate in the classroom: A handbook for teachers.* Washington, DC: Center for Applied Linguistics.

Southwest Educational Development Laboratory. (2003). *SEDL helps parents prepare for parent–teacher conferences* (press release). Austin, TX: Author.

Retrieved November 18, 2004, from www.sedl.org/new/pressrelease/20031001_16.html.

Tang, G. M. (1994). Textbook illustrations: A cross-cultural study and its implications for teachers of language minority students. *Journal of Educational Issues of Language Minority Students*, 175–194.

Thornbury, S. (1999). *How to teach grammar*. Harlow, UK: Pearson Education Limited.

U.S. Department of Education, National Center for Education Statistics. (n.d.). *Schools and staffing survey: 1999–2000*. Retrieved July 16, 2005, from http://nces.ed.gov/pubs2002/2002313.pdf.

U.S. Department of Education, National Center for Education Statistics. (2005). *The condition of education 2005*. Retrieved July 15, 2005, from http://nces.ed.gov/programs/coe/2005/section1/indicator05.asp.

Valdes, G. (1996). *Con respeto: Bridging the distance between culturally diverse families and schools: An ethnographic portrait*. New York: Teachers College Press.

Vygotsky, L. S. (1978). *Mind and society*. Cambridge, MA: Harvard University Press.

Wong Fillmore, L., & Snow, C. E. (2000). *What teachers need to know about language*. Washington, DC: Department of Education. (ERIC Document Reproduction Service No. ED 990 008).

Wright, S. P., Horn, S. P., & Sanders, W. L. (1997). Teacher and classroom context effects on student achievement: Implications for teacher evaluation. *Journal of Personnel Evaluation in Education, 11*, 57–67.

Zehler, A. (1994, Summer). Working with English language learners: Strategies for elementary and middle school teachers. *NCELA Program Information Guide Series* (No. 19).

INDEX

ability, relationship to achievement, 11
achievement. *See also* effort, reinforcing
    academic vs. conversational profi-
      ciency, 16–18, 17*f*, 102
    beliefs about, mistaken, 11
    note taking and, 70
    strategies for increasing, 5–13
achievement rubrics, 88, 89–90*f*
advance organizers
    adapting for ELLs, 49–54
    expository, 8, 49
    generalizations from the research on,
      8, 48–49
    graphic, 8, 52–54, 53*f*
    narrative, 8, 50–51
    purpose of, 48
    skimming as a form of, 8, 51–52
    summary, 54
    types of, 8, 48
affective filter hypothesis, 87
argumentation frame, 125
Asher, James, 40
assessment, feedback for, 33
attribute charts, 104–106, 104*f*

Bailey, Cecilia, 57–58

Berry, Elisabeth, 40
BICS (basic interpersonal communica-
    tive skills), 17

clarifying, in reciprocal teaching, 66, 69
Classroom Instruction That Works
    (Marzano, Pickering, & Pollock), on
    advance organizers, 48–52
    cooperative learning, 57–58
    cues and questions, 46–48, 47*f*
    feedback, 32–34
    generating and testing hypotheses,
      95, 97
    homework, 78–79
    identifying similarities and differ-
      ences, 101–104
    introduction, 3–4, 6
    K-W-L charts, 47*f*
    nonlinguistic representations, 37–41
    note taking, 69–70, 70–71
    objective setting, 28
    practice, 84–85
    recognizing students, 92–94
    reinforcing effort, 88, 89–90*f*
    setting objectives, 27–28
    summarizing, 63–66

Cognitive Academic Language Learning Approach (CALLA), 62
cognitive academic language proficiency (CALP), 17
communication
    basic skills of (BICS), 17
    cognition and context in, 102
    conversational vs. academic proficiency, 16–18, 17*f*, 102
    conversation frame, 125
community involvement, 111–117, 113*f*, 127–130
comparison matrix, similarities vs. differences, 106, 108*f*, 110*f*
content ESL. *See* instruction, sheltered
cues and questions. *See also* questions
    adapting for ELLs, 46–48, 47*f*
    explicit, 47
    generalizations from the research on, 7–8, 46
    purpose of, 44–45
summary, 54
    Cummins, Jim, 102

Daigler, Sheri, 71
definition frame, 64, 65*f*
differences, identifying. *See* similarities and differences, identifying
drama class, 41
Dreschler, Sandra, 65

early production ELLs, and
    cooperative learning, 59
    effort-achievement rubrics, 88, 89–90*f*, 91
    explicit cues and background knowledge, 47
    feedback, 34
    generating and testing hypotheses, 96, 99
    graphic advance organizers, 42, 54
    homework, 80, 82, 82*f*
    identifying similarities and differences, 103, 104, 106, 108
    keep-delete-substitute strategy, 63, 67
    language acquisition stages, 15*f*
    nonlinguistic representations, 37
    note taking, 75
    practice, 85
    praise or recognition, 93, 94
    questioning to elicit inferences, 47
    reciprocal teaching, 69
    setting language objectives, 30
    skimming strategy, 52

early production ELLs—(*continued*)
    summary frames, 68
    teacher-prepared notes, 71
    teaching text structure and patterns, 63
    Word-MES strategy, 19, 60
effort, reinforcing
    adapting for ELLs, 88, 89–90*f*, 91–92, 91*f*
    generalizations from the research on, 11, 88
    purpose of, 87
    rubrics for, 88, 89–90*f*
    summary, 94
ELLs, statistics on
    ages 5–17 years, xii
    in homes without English spoken, xii, 2
    increases (1979-2003), 2, 3
    preK–3, xii, 3
    regional distributions, 2
    teacher training, 118
    time required for proficiency, 17, 18
emotion, language acquisition and negative, 56–57, 87
English, academic vs. conversational, 16–18, 17*f*, 102
Epstein, Joyce, 112
error correction, 31–32
ESL content. *See* instruction, sheltered
expectations, rubrics and, 33
expository advance organizers, 8, 49

feedback
    adapting for ELLs, 33–35
    effective forms of, 31–32
    generalizations from the research on, 6–7, 32
    on homework assignments, 79
    matching oral and written corrective, 34–35
    peer vs. teacher, 34, 56
    question-response-feedback pattern, 45
    small groups and, 56
    student-led, 34
    summary, 35
    written language, 33, 33*f*
fluency ELLs, intermediate and advanced, and
    cooperative learning, 60
    effort-achievement rubrics, 89–90*f*, 92
    explicit cues and background knowledge, 47

fluency ELLs—(*continued*)
    feedback, 35
    generating and testing hypotheses, 97, 99
    graphic advance organizers, 43, 54
    homework, 80, 83
    identifying similarities and differences, 103, 104, 107, 108
    keep-delete-substitute strategy, 63, 67
    language acquisition stages, 15*f*
    note taking, 76
    practice, 84, 85
    praise or recognition, 94
    questioning to elicit inferences, 47
    reciprocal teaching, 69
    setting language objectives, 30–31
    skimming, 52
    summary frames, 68
    teacher-prepared notes, 72
    teaching text structure and patterns, 63
    Word-MES strategy, 20, 60
frame questions, 64, 123–126

Gardner, Kelly, 41
geometry class, 41
Gibson, William, 38
goal setting. *See* objective setting
grading, rubrics and, 33
graphic organizers
    as advance organizers, 8, 52–54, 53*f*
    example, 41–43, 42*f*
    for generating hypotheses, 98*f*
    identifying similarities and differences with, 104
    types of, 38, 121–122*f*
group learning. *See* learning, cooperative

A Handbook for Classroom Instruction That Works (Marzano, Pickering, & Pollock), 6
history class, 41
Hitchcock, Denise, 40
Hodgkinson, Harold, xii
homework. *See also* practice
    adapting for ELLs, 78, 79, 80–83, 81*f*, 82*f*, 83*f*
    generalizations from the research on, 10, 10–11, 78–79
    online resources for, 77–78
    parental involvement in, 78–79
    purpose of, 79
    summary, 86
    tips for ensuring completion of, 77–78

hypotheses, generating and testing
    adapting for ELLs, 96–99, 98*f*
    generalizations from the research on, 11–12, 95
    summary, 99–100

if-then reasoning, 95
inferences, questions to elicit, 47
instruction, sheltered, 24–25, 44
instructional strategies, defined, 5–6
"In the Classroom: A Toolkit for Effective Instruction of English Learners" (NCELA), 65, 77
"In the Classroom: Guiding Principles" (NCELA), 78

keep-delete-substitute strategy, 63, 66–67
key concepts, 27
kinesthetic activities, representing knowledge with, 39–41. *See also* senses, using all the
knowledge. *See also* nonlinguistic representations
    background, 44, 47, 47*f*, 69
    linguistic, 36
Krashen, Stephen, 14, 15, 87
K-W-L charts, 47*f*

language
    academic vs. conversational, 16–18, 17*f*, 23, 102
    function and structures, determining, 25–28, 31
    introduction, 1–2
    teaching, elements of, 2
    written, 33, 33*f*
language acquisition. *See also* specific stages of
    academic proficiency and, 16–18, 17*f*
    feedback effective for, 31–32
    instructional adaptation example, 18–19
    negative emotions and, 56–57, 87
    requirements for ensuring, 56
    scaffolding for, 16, 33–34, 45–46
    stages of, 14–16, 15*f*
    summary, 20
    Word-MES strategy, 19–20
learning
    cooperative
        adapting for ELLs, 57–61
        advantages to ELLs, 56–57
        elements specific to, 55
        generalizations from the research on, 9, 57

learning—(*continued*)
    introduction, 9
    summary, 61
    questions most effective for, 46
Libertini, Amy, 102
luck, achievement and, 11

manipulatives, representing knowledge
    with, 39
maps and diagrams, 38
mastery, 84
mental pictures for representing knowl-
    edge, 38
models, representing knowledge with, 39
Moses, Lindsay, 39

narrative advance organizers, 8, 50–51
narrative frame, 123–124
National Center for Research on Educa-
    tion, Diversity & Excellence, 24
National Clearinghouse for English Lan-
    guage Acquisition (NCELA), 3
The Natural Approach (Krashen &
    Terrell), 14
No Child Left Behind Act (NCLB), 5,
    22–23, 24, 114
nonlinguistic representations. *See also*
    graphic organizers
    adapting for ELLs, 36–43
    generalizations from the research on,
        7, 37
    identifying similarities and differ-
        ences with, 102–103
    kinesthetic activities, 39–41
    mental pictures, 38
    in note taking, 70
    summary, 43
    symbolic representations, 38, 39f, 40f
notes, teacher-prepared, 70, 71–72, 75f
note taking
    adapting for ELLs, 70–71
    formats, types of, 72f, 73–74f, 75f
    generalizations from the research on,
        9–10, 69–70
    summary, 76

objective setting
    adapting for ELLs, 28–31, 29f
    generalizations from the research on,
        6–7, 27–28
    language and content integration for,
        23–27
    purpose of, 22
    summary, 35
organizers. *See* advance organizers;
    graphic organizers

parental involvement
    in homework, 78–79
    six types of, 113f
    three-year plan example, 127–130
pause-prompt-praise strategy, 93
pictographs and pictures, 38, 39f, 40f
practice. *See also* homework
    adapting for ELLs, 85–86
    generalizations from the research on,
        10–11, 84
    purpose of, 83–84
    summary, 86
praise, performance and, 92–93
predicting, in reciprocal teaching, 66, 69
preproduction ELLs, and
    cooperative learning, 59
    effort-achievement rubrics, 88,
        89–90f, 91
    explicit cues and background knowl-
        edge, 47
    feedback, 34
    generating and testing hypotheses,
        96, 98
    graphic advance organizers, 42,
        53–54
    homework, 80, 81–82, 81f
    identifying similarities and differ-
        ences, 102, 103, 104, 106, 108
    keep-delete-substitute strategy, 63,
        66
    language acquisition stages, 15f
    nonlinguistic representations, 37
    note taking, 74
    practice, 85
    praise or recognition, 93, 94
    questioning to elicit inferences, 47
    reciprocal teaching, 69
    setting language objectives, 29–30
    skimming strategy, 52
    summary frames, 68
    teacher-prepared notes, 71
    teaching text structure and patterns,
        63
    Word-MES strategy, 19, 60
Problem-solution frame, 125
professional development, 31

question-answer patterns, 45
questions. *See also* cues and questions
    analytic, 48
    to elicit inferences, 47
    frame completion
        argumentation, 125
        conversation, 125
        definition, 64

questions—(*continued*)
  narrative, 124
  problem/solution, 125
  topic-restriction-illustration, 124
  in reciprocal teaching, 66, 68
  tiered form for scaffolding, 16,
    33–34, 45

Ramirez Report (Ramirez), 16
reasoning, inductive and deductive, 95
recognition
  abstract, 92–93
  adapting for ELLs, 93–94
  concrete symbols of, 93–94
  generalizations from the research on,
    11, 92–93
  pause-prompt-praise strategy, 93
  personalized, 93, 94
  summary, 94
rubrics
  for effort and achievement, 88, 89f
  for feedback, 33
  student-created, 33

scaffolding, 16, 33–34
Schmucker, Adam, 52
school quality relationship to achievement, 5
SDAIE (specially designed academic
  instruction in English). *See* instruction, sheltered
Segal, Berty, 40
self-confidence and language acquisition,
  87
senses, using all the, 38. *See also* kinesthetic activities, representing knowledge with
Sheltered Instruction Observation Protocol (SIOP), 24–25, 44
sheltering techniques, 24, 49–50
similarities and differences, identifying
  adapting for ELLs, 103–109, 104f,
    106f, 107f, 108f, 109f
  attribute charts for, 104–106, 104f
  comparison matrix for, 106, 108f,
    110f
  forms of, 103
  generalizations from the research on,
    12, 101–103
  summary, 109
  tips for facilitating, 102
  Venn diagrams in, 106–107, 106f,
    107f
skimming, 8, 51–52
Sorte, Eliza, 52

speech emergence ELLs, and
  cooperative learning, 60
  effort-achievement rubrics, 89–90f,
    91
  explicit cues and background knowl-
    edge, 47
  feedback, 35
  generating and testing hypotheses,
    96–97, 99
  graphic advance organizers, 43, 54
  homework, 80, 82, 83f
  identifying similarities and differ-
    ences, 103, 104, 107, 108
  keep-delete-substitute strategy, 63,
    67
  language acquisition stages, 15f
  note taking, 75
  practice, 85
  praise or recognition, 94
  questioning to elicit inferences, 47
  reciprocal teaching, 69
  setting language objectives, 30
  skimming strategy, 52
  summary frames, 68
  teacher-prepared notes, 71
  teaching text structure and patterns,
    63
  Word-MES strategy, 19, 60
story frame, 123–124
student performance. *See* achievement
summarizing
  generalizations from the research on,
    9, 63
  keep-delete-substitute strategy, 63,
    66–67
  in reciprocal teaching, 65–66, 68–69
  rule-based strategy, 63–64
  summary, 76
summary frames, 64, 67–68, 123–126
Survey, Question, Read, Recite, and
  Review (SQ3R) strategy, 51–52
symbolic representations of information,
  38, 39f, 40f

teachers influence on achievement, 5
teaching, reciprocal, 64–65, 68–69
Teaching English Through Action (Segal),
  40
Terrell, Tracy, 14, 15, 87
test study guides, 70
text structure and patterns, 63–65
Thornbury, S., 31
topic-restriction-illustration frame, 124
Total Physical Response (TPR), 39–40

Venn diagrams, 106–107, 106f, 107f
visual representations. *See* nonlinguistic
    representations
vocabulary acquisition, 19–20, 21f. *See
    also* Word-MES strategy
vocabulary instruction, 27
Vygotsky, L. S., 16

wait time as questioning strategy, 46
Word-MES strategy, 19–20, 34–35, 60
word walls, 20, 21f

zone of proximal development, 16

ABOUT THE AUTHORS

Jane D. Hill, a lead consultant for Mid-continent Research for Education and Learning (McREL), has worked in the areas of second language acquisition and special education for 25 years and consults and trains nationally with teachers and administrators. Prior to joining McREL, Jane worked as a Speech/  Language Specialist for 13 years specializing in bilingual special education. She directed a two-way language school for three years and served as district director for second language acquisition and special education for seven years. She earned her BA from Simpson College in Iowa in theater arts/speech and her MS from Colorado State University in communication disorders. She has recently written for *Language Magazine* and contributed to the second edition of the CD-ROM, *Making Schools Work for Every Child* (Eisenhower National Clearinghouse for Mathematics and Science Education, 2005). Jane also conducts training in *Teaching Reading in the Content Areas* and *Classroom Instruction That Works*. She can be contacted at jhill@mcrel.org.

Kathleen M. Flynn is a senior consultant at McREL, where she shares management responsibilities for McREL's regional educational laboratory contract. In this position, she is responsible for helping McREL staff write and revise laboratory publications. Most recently, she cowrote (with Jane Hill) a resource guide titled *English Language Learner Resource Guide: A Guide for Rural Districts with a Low Incidence of ELLs* (McREL, 2004). This document was based on McREL's recent work with a rural Wyoming school district that has encountered a growing number of ELLs in its student population.

Prior to joining McREL, Kathleen spent seven years as a practicing attorney and also worked as an elementary school teacher. She received a BA cum laude in English and philosophy from Mount Holyoke College in 1985 and a JD from Northwestern University School of Law in 1994, and she is currently on track to receive an MA in educational psychology from the University of Colorado in 2006. She can be contacted at kflynn@mcrel.org.

Related ASCD Resources: English Language Learners

At the time of publication, the following ASCD resources were available; for the most up-to-date information about ASCD resources, go to www.ascd.org. ASCD stock numbers are noted in parentheses.

Audio

Active Learning for Teachers: Success for English Learners
    by Adrienne Herrell and Michael Jordan (#204249S25)
Best Practices for Powerful Learning for English Language Learners
    by Fay Mpras and Shirley Thomas (#204226S25)
English Language Learners: What Do Teachers Need to Know?
    by Catherine Snow (#505360S25)

Books

Classroom Instruction That Works: Research-Based Strategies for Increasing Student Achievement by Robert J. Marzano,
    Debra J. Pickering and Jane E. Pollock (#101010)
Meeting the Needs of Second Language Learners: An Educator's Guide
    by Judith Lessow-Hurley (#102043S25)

Video

Maximizing Learning for English Language Learners Entire Series
    [three videocassettes] (#403326S25)
A Visit to a Classroom of English Language Learners (#404447S25)

For more information, visit us on the World Wide Web (http://www.ascd.org), send an e-mail message to member@ascd.org, call the ASCD Service Center (1-800-933-ASCD or 703-578-9600, then press 2), send a fax to 703-575-5400, or write to Information Services, ASCD, 1703 N. Beauregard St., Alexandria, VA 22311-1714 USA.